LUCY CALKINS

A GUIDE TO THE WRITING WORKSHOP, GRADES 3-5

This book is dedicated to John Skorpen, my life partner, with love.

FirstHand
An imprint of Heinemann
A division of Reed Elsevier Inc.
361 Hanover Street
Portsmouth, NH 03801-3912
www.heinemann.com

Offices and agents throughout the world

Photography: Peter Cunningham

Library of Congress Cataloging-in-Publication Data

CIP data on file with the Library of Congress.
ISBN 0-325-00861-2

Printed in the United States of America on acid-free paper
10   09   08   07   06   ML   2   3   4   5

ACKNOWLEDGEMENTS

This series has the biggest undertaking of my life—other than the larger projects of leading the Teachers College Reading and Writing Project and of parenting Miles and Evan—and so it is fitting that I dedicate this project to John Skorpen, who has been my life partner through it all. There have been lots of books before now, but John is the sort of person to say, "Dedicate that one to your parents," or "Have you remembered…?" Just this once, I want to say to John and to the world that I am the luckiest person alive because I am married to someone who understands and cherishes me, who knows that my work gives me great joy, who cares for the family as much as I do, and who is always glad that we can come home to each other. John, thanks for your depth of understanding, your wise observations, your spirit of adventure, your sense of priorities, your forgiveness and your love.

When I write and when I teach, I reach through words to something that is deeper, older, purer than words…and I know that the source, way down deep inside of me, has everything to do with my mother and my father, and with the legacy of my family. I thank both Evan and Virginia Calkins for all that I am, for all that I believe in, and I thank each of my eight brothers and sisters—Sally, Steve, Joan, Ben, Hugh, Ellen, Geoff, and Tim— for understanding the preciousness of family.

Anyone who has ever read my writing or been part of my teaching knows that the sun rises and sets for me with Miles and Evan Skorpen, my two beloved sons who are now becoming young men. John and I could not be more proud of them.

I live and learn as part of the community of teacher-educators that comprises the Teachers College Reading and Writing Project, and there are a few people at the Project who have been especially important thought-companions. I especially thank Laurie Pessah, who has always helped me lead the organization, Kathleen Tolan and Mary Ehrenworth, Deputy Directors, Ruth Swinney, Director of English Language Learners,

and Beth Neville, Associate Director. For the past year, this leadership team has been coached by a leader-of-leaders, Patsy Glazer, and we are all grateful to her. I am also grateful to Amanda Hartman who demonstrates what is possible in staff development, for Maggie Moon for assuming a leadership role at the Project, and for Brooke Keller who has helped me think more deeply.

The ideas about teaching writing that are essential in this book were introduced to me when I was a young teacher and I am eternally grateful to Don Graves and Don Murray for being my first mentors in the teaching of writing. Since then, I've learned from many others. Randy Bomer, author of *Time for Meaning* and former President of the National Council of Teachers of English, has been an especially important influence, and his insights and suggestions helped me create a form for and imagine these books. Many former Teachers College Reading and Writing Project colleagues—including Shelley Harwayne, Joanne Hindley, JoAnne Portalupi, Ralph Fletcher, Georgia Heard, Isoke Nia, Katherine Bomer, Katie Ray, Pam Allyn, and Carl Anderson— added layers of insight to my knowledge on teaching writing.

I am grateful to the co-authors who joined me in writing these books. Colleen Cruz has been a wonderful writing partner, and her ideas and experience at writing fiction made that book into what it is. Mary Chiarella not only contributed to the final book in the series, but has also been the teacher I rely upon most in all of these books. Her children's work stud the pages of every book, and I salute her for being Writing Teacher Extraordinaire. Kathy Collins, co-author of the CD-ROM, is a whiz at anything demanding creativity, energy, an intimate knowledge of the very real world of classroom teaching. I thank her for her gigantic contribution. I am also thankful to the contributing authors, each of whom pitched in on a particular book; I describe their contributions in those books.

Because of the scale of this writing effort, I recruited a few others to help me. Julia Mooney has brought her sparkling intelligence and her deep understanding of good writing to the pages of every book. She especially helped contributing and co-authors authors write their Tailoring your Teachings. Natalie Louis, Shannon Rigney Keane, Grace Enriquez and Kathy Doyle each helped as well. Katherine Bomer brought her special verve and her sense of intimacy with kids and texts to some of these books. Ruth Swinney provided invaluable assistance with the chapter on supporting English Language learners. Peter Cunningham, the photographer for these books and for every book I've ever written, graced this effort with magical talent.

The book stands on the shoulders of the Teachers Reading and Writing Project's alliance with the New York City schools, and that alliance relies upon a close relationship with Regional Superintendents and Deputy Superintendents. I especially thank Judy Chin and Brenda Steele from Region 3, Reyes Irizarry and Charles Amundsen from Region 4, Peter Heaney and Barbara Gambino from Region 9, and Marcia Lyles and Elaine Goldberg from Region 8. Their work relies upon leadership from Chancellor Joel Klein, Deputy Chancellor Carmen Farina and Director of Instruction, Laura Kotch.

Leigh Peake has led Heinemann's involvement with this effort, and I thank her both for channeling enormous support towards this project and for her responsiveness to me. With Leigh at the helm of Heinemann, the organization is able to maintain its very special identity as a think tank and a family as well as a service-provider. Jean Lawler has been the production mastermind at Heinemann. She has kept track of all the zillions of bits and pieces that create the mosaic of these books, and worked with terrific dedication and good will. Jean has been utterly and completely essential to the entire process. She's been lucky to have support from David Stirling. Charles McQuillen will take over once Jean

has let go, and I thank him in advance for what he will do to usher the books into the hands of teachers.

Most of all, I am grateful to Kate Montgomery. Whereas John is my life-partner, Kate is my writing partner. I could not have written these books without her brilliant presence at my side. Kate cares as much as I do; her standards are sky-high, and she has the talent to see and to bring forth the lion that is hiding, still, deep in the marble. I've dedicated *Launching the Writing Workshop* to her— a small gesture when her name really deserves to be on the cover of each book!

A Guide to the Writing Workshop, Grades 3-5

CHAPTER 1

ABOUT THE SERIES

This is the first in a series of books designed to help upper-elementary teachers teach a rigorous yearlong writing curriculum. The series stands on the shoulders of the Teachers College Reading and Writing Project community. The books have, in a sense, been coauthored by the entire staff of this professional development organization and by the teachers, principals, and superintendents who have become part of the community of practice, helping develop, pilot, and revise the ideas that fill the pages of these books.

Together, all of us have passed the baton to others, helping several hundred thousand teachers become skilled at teaching writing. Word has spread. Over the years, more and more teachers have heard that the writing workshop has given children unbelievable power as readers, thinkers, and composers of meaning—and that it has given *teachers* new energy and joy, reminding us why we chose careers in teaching in the first place. Demand for support in the teaching of writing has skyrocketed. This series is my effort to provide that support.

The increased focus on writing comes in part from the technological revolution that has transformed our lives. As the Internet and text messaging seep into every nook and cranny of our day, all of us are writing more than ever. In today's Information Age, it has become increasingly important that all children are given an education that enables them to synthesize, organize, reflect on, and respond to the data in their world. Indeed, three years ago, a National Writing Commission called for a Writing Revolution, suggesting that children need to double the amount of time they spend writing in their classrooms.

But above all, the escalating demand for professional development in the teaching of writing comes because when teachers receive the education we deserve in the teaching of writing and are therefore able to provide children with clear, sequenced, vibrant instruction in writing (along with opportunities to write daily for their own important purposes), we make a dramatic difference in children's abilities to write. The stories and essays that children produce as a result become far more substantial and significant, revealing the young authors in ways that are often poignant.

Strong writing instruction can also power dramatic increases in scores on standardized tests. Today, students need to write well to achieve on the SAT and on advanced placement exams. More and more states have either integrated writing into their standardized reading tests or added separate assessments of writing.

Educators who wonder whether adopting a reading and writing workshop will translate into increases in standardized tests will want to notice the impressive gains New York City has made since the Chancellor held a press conference at P.S. 172, a Teachers College Reading and Writing Project stronghold, in which he said that the approach in that school needed to be taken citywide. Since adopting balanced literacy, New York City's test scores have skyrocketed, with double-digit increases in state standardized tests in grades three, four and five. The most important gains in New York City have been on the NAEP, often referred to as the "nation's report card." This assessment is mandated by Congress and administered by the US Department of Education. Last December, recent NAEP scores were released showing that New York City's fourth grade school students outperformed their peers in other cities with populations over 250,000.

Sheila Ford, Vice Chair of the National Assessment Governing Board of the NAEP was quoted in a recent Education Week article saying, "New York City had the greatest gains of any urban city setting in the country in the area of reading." In a speech to the principals and superintendents from schools across the country which are affiliated with the Project, she elaborated saying, "The important thing to realize is that over thirty years, the NAEP scores nationally have been essentially flat. Since New York City adopted the balanced literacy approach citywide in 2002, New York City's scores have risen 7 points which is a statistically significant gain. New York City is also the largest school district in the nation with 1.1 million students, and 84 percent of its fourth graders are eligible for free or reduced lunch." New York is making progress bridging the achievement gap. New York City's Black and Hispanic low income fourth graders far outperformed similar students in large cities and in the nation as a whole on the percentage of students achieving at or above the basic level.

NAEP writing scores for major cities will be released in 2007 but even before the writing workshop was extended citywide, New York City children wrote better than children in any other major city except Charlotte. More generally, data from the NAEP assessment show clearly that children who are accustomed to writing more than one draft and who save their writing in folders—techniques that are hallmarks of a writing workshop—perform better as writers than do other students.

Although it is reassuring to realize that teaching children to write well can transfer into improved scores on standardized tests, those of us who put writing at the center of our professional lives do so for far more personal and compelling reasons. First of all, it is not only *children's* work that is transformed through professional development in the teaching of writing; *teachers'* work is also transformed. When a community of teachers embraces reform in the teaching of writing, teachers often become reinvigorated and renewed in the process. And individual teachers find that teaching writing taps new sources of energy within themselves. Over the years, teachers have continually told me that the teaching of writing has given them new energy, clarity, and compassion, reminding them why they went into teaching in the first place. I understand what these teachers mean, for writing has done all this—and more—for me.

Lifting the level of writing instruction matters because writing matters. I recently read an article that reminded me of the human need to tell and write the stories of our lives. The article was about Ivory, a man whose job had been to drive a garbage truck through New Orleans and who was, at the time of the article, living on a cot in the New Orleans Convention Center and had only a small cardboard box full of salvaged stuff left to show for his life. Sitting on that cot, bereft of all that he'd built for himself, Ivory asked to borrow a pencil and then began listing everything he'd lost in Hurricane Katrina: the framed photograph of his mother, the radio that had turned his little apartment into a pub, the table he'd found once beside the road . . . . I'm quite sure that as Ivory recorded each precious item on his page, it was as if those items were, in some way, still a part of him: "This is me," he seemed to be saying. Writing is a way for us to hold onto the moments and the selves that could otherwise slip through our fingers.

All of us rush through our lives: we wake up, we eat our breakfast, we hurry to school, into our classroom, we hang up our coat, we wave hello to this person and that, time passes and soon one day becomes the next. Behind us, we leave what John Updike calls "a litter of old selves." Ten-year-old Geirthruder wrote:

> I often think that my life is like a handful of sand, they fall, there's nothing you can do about it, it will keep falling until it's all gone, which is why I hate digital watches that count seconds.

Of course, no one is leaving behind old selves in faster, more dramatic ways than children. It is children who know the glee, and the sadness, too, of finding they can no longer squeeze through the gap in the backyard fence. It is children who find their voices changing, their legs getting longer. It is children who constantly outgrow trousers and roles. And children, like adults, need ways to set their lives onto the page, to hold on to their past and make meaning in their present.

It is not enough simply to go from here to there, from this moment to that one. We need our moments and our days to add up, to mean something, to cumulate. As Ernst Becker has said, "What human beings fear is not growing old, but growing old without things adding up." And so we write.

We write to hold on to the moments of our lives and to make them matter. Patricia MacLachlan, the Newbery Medal–winning author of *Journey*, writes, "Other animals have journeys far greater than ours. The arctic tern crisscrosses the Atlantic Ocean many times. The monarch butterfly summers in the meadows of Maine and winters in the rain forests of Mexico." Then she adds, "But we are the creature that lives to tell the tale." During prehistoric times, human beings used whatever we could find—sticks, berries, pieces of rock—to record the stories of our hunts and journeys on stony cave walls. Then, standing in the company of one another, we reread, recalled, reconsidered the hunts and journeys that we'd been on and imagined the ones still before us. I am convinced this is how we human beings became human. We live through our days, and then we turn back and say, "This is my journey, and this is what I make of it." In the end, each and every one of us is the author of a life: *My Life*, we each write. *My Life*, by me.

We've written this series because writing matters. Demand for professional development in writing has far outstripped the Teachers College Reading and Writing Project's abilities to provide this support. These books reflect our effort to hand over what we know so that more children can be given opportunities to grow strong as writers and more teachers can experience the extraordinary benefits that come from participating in a community of practice that involves a shared inquiry into the teaching of writing.

The wonderful thing about learning to teach writing well is that there are just a few teaching methods that one needs to know and be able to use. In this series, I provide crystal-clear advice on how to lead efficient and effective minilessons, conferences, and small-group strategy sessions. I do so knowing that as you travel through the series, encountering scores of transcripts of minilessons, conferences, small-group sessions, and shares, you will learn not only from explicit instruction but also from immersion. This first book of the series explicitly describes the architecture of all our minilessons, conferences, and small-group strategy sessions and details the management techniques that make writing workshops possible. The subsequent books show these methods and principles effecting real life in classrooms. I know from helping thousands of teachers learn to teach writing that these units will scaffold and inform your own teaching, and you will develop finesse and flexibility with the methods and information conveyed in these books.

In an ideal world, every teacher deserves the chance to learn state-of-the-art methods for teaching writing not only by reading books but also by watching an exemplary teacher instruct her children day to day. Although we do not live in an ideal world, teachers who have relied on the *Units of Study for Primary Writing* (or on the binders containing very early and incomplete preliminary versions of the upper grade units) will assure you that these books can be a next-best substitute. They can give you the chance to listen in on and observe my teaching and, at times, the teaching of one of my colleagues. Each unit of study in this series contains the words of my teaching (and sometimes of a colleague's teaching) for between fifteen and twenty days, with suggested ways to extend each of those days if this seems merited. You will read the words I used to gather a class of students together on the rug for a minilesson, and then, once the children are gathered, you'll hear exactly what I said to them. You will hear me retell a harrowing moment with my dog, Tucker, and you'll see how I use that anecdote to illustrate a quality of good writing.

Ideally, you and every other teacher in the world should be able not only to observe exemplary teachers but also to do so with a coach nearby, highlighting the way the teaching illustrates a collection of guiding principles. Ideally, someone will be there at your side to point out the alternative decisions the teacher could and could not have made in any one moment. Therefore, as you witness this teaching, I will be an ever-present coach, highlighting aspects of the teaching that seem especially essential. My goal is to help you watch this teaching in ways that enable you to extrapolate guidelines and methods, so that on another day you'll invent your own teaching.

I already know, from talking with so many teachers who've used the *Units of Study for Primary Writing,* that sometimes you will take the words of my minilessons and bring them verbatim to your own children. I also know that more often you'll decide that the teaching I describe needs to be adapted or rewritten in order to fit you and your children. These books provide a detailed model; they are not meant as a script. Either way, the end goal is not the teaching that I've described here but the teaching that you, your colleagues, and your children invent together.

The most important thing for you to know is that the books are designed to put themselves out of a job. Once you have used this scaffold to support your teaching, you will find you no longer need it. You will see that your students need more help with one strategy or another, and you'll use the principles in these books to help you author minilessons, small-group work, and conferences tailored to the needs of your students. This series supports only six or seven months of teaching writing. In order to provide your children with a *yearlong* curriculum in writing, you will need to create your own units of study with your colleagues; these books will help you to do so.

The books are intended to be read and used in sequence, each book standing on the shoulders of the books that go before it. (The order of *Fiction* and *Literary Essays* could conceivably be flipped; other than that, they must proceed in order.) A few homemade units can be inserted between the fifth and the sixth book. I suggest one of these be a unit of study on poetry, and I will later direct you to sources of support for that unit and others. Together, these units (including the ones you author yourself) will combine to provide the curricular support necessary to take a class of upper elementary students on a learning journey. The series can also provide the backbone for a second or third year of study, as long as teachers in the succeeding years are increasingly willing to tailor their teaching to take into account what children already know and can do. That is, children profit from a spiral curriculum in writing: for example, in third grade they learn to write detailed, chronological personal narratives, but then in fourth grade, they have opportunities to deepen their knowledge of narrative writing. Because the teaching in these books is highly predictable, and because each bit of it draws on principles that are clearly articulated, you will find that these books will take not only your students but also you and your colleagues on a learning journey.

The Parts of Each Session

Here is what you can expect in each of the fifteen or so sessions in each unit book in this series.

Getting Ready

This list can help you be sure you have the materials you need for each minilesson. Further detail is included on the CD-ROM. The required materials are kept to a minimum!

Introduction

Just as minilessons begin with Lucy pulling children close to tell them what the upcoming lesson aims to teach, to explain how this lesson fits with previous ones and to convey why the teaching matters, so, too, each session begins with Lucy doing the same for you.

Minilesson

Listen in while Lucy teaches. Hear the language she uses and hear, also, some of what children say in response. These won't provide scripts for your teaching because the lessons are tailored to a particular class of children, but you can learn from and adapt them. Each minilesson follows the same architecture:

Connection: Children learn why today's instruction is important and how it relates to their prior work. They hear the teaching point that crystallizes the lesson.

Teaching: The teacher shows children how writers go about doing whatever is being taught. Usually this involves a demonstration, which the teacher sets up and explains.

Active Engagement: Children are given a chance to practice (for a minute) what has just been taught. The teacher scaffolds their work so they can be successful.

Link: The teacher crystallizes what has been taught, adding it to children's growing repertoire. Children are reminded that today's lesson pertains not only to today, but to every day. The teacher often summarizes the conditions under which a child to reach for this new knowledge.

Italicized Commentary: As you read and picture the teaching, Lucy will coach you to realize why she's taught the way she has, to see other choices she could have made, to notice the aspects of today's teaching which are transferable to other days, to understand ways one day's teaching stands on the shoulders of previous days, and to consider ways the teaching could be adapted for children with different needs.

WRITING AND CONFERRING

Although children always catch us by surprise when we draw a chair alongside them to confer, the truth is our conferences are not as off-the-cuff as they may seem. Experienced teachers of writing can plan a minilesson and predict the coaching and instruction children will especially need. It is predictable, too, that some days children will need so much help that it will be important to devote the workshop to small group instruction. In some of these sessions, you will listen in on the conferences or small groups that Lucy led in the wake of that day's minilesson. Other times, this session will equip you to lead the conferences or small group work that are apt to be especially helpful that day.

MID-WORKSHOP
TEACHING POINT

It is inevitable that in the midst of a writing workshop, a teacher will want to interrupt the hum of the workshop to teach the entire class. Often this teaching builds upon the minilesson. Most mid-workshop teaching points are actually mini-minilessons!

SHARE

Every writing workshop ends with a share. This provides one more opportunity to sneak in some pointers. Usually during the share, Lucy will highlight one child's work in a way that create a trail that others could follow, and then she'll channel each child towards a productive conversation with his or her writing partner.

HOMEWORK AND LETTERS TO PARENTS

By the time children are in the upper elementary grades, they can do substantial work at home, and they will be more eager to do this work if we are careful to craft homework that helps children outgrow themselves. Each session, then, contains two or sometimes three different variations of homework assignments. These are written to be read by children. They always include a pep-talk (a miniature minilesson) and sometimes include exemplar work. The homework section provides you with a way to communicate with parents about the important work children are doing in school. In addition, the CD also contains letters that can be sent home to parents describing each unit of study. You'll want to alter both the homework and the letters, and so they are packaged to make it easy for you to do so.

TAILORING YOUR TEACHING

With adaptations, the lessons that you read in these sessions can provide the backbone for your own units of study, but you will want to tailor your teaching based on what you see your children needing. After each session, then, there is a description of minilesson extensions. Here and on the CD, Lucy Calkins, Kathy Collins and the contributing authors and co-authors imagine ways in which your children may need further help. "If this is the second time your children are traveling through the unit…" we may write, and then suggest the kernel of a minilesson you might give to them. "If your children are struggling with…" we may say, and again suggest a minilesson. Each session provides a handful of extensions, some in the book and more on the CD.

ASSESSMENT/MECHANICS/COLLABORATING WITH COLLEAGUES

These three strands are woven through each of the units of study, with a 1-2 page discussion of one of these topics at the end of each session. The mechanics section suggests ways in which you can teach the conventions of writing both within and outside the writing workshop. Collaborating with Colleagues suggests ways that you and your colleagues can use study-group time productively in support of this unit. Assessment suggests lenses you might use as this particular time in your children's development, and helps you imagine ways to make sense of what you will probably see.

THE FOUNDATIONS OF A WRITING WORKSHOP

Whenever I work with educators in a school, a school district, or a city, I make a point of meeting with educational leaders to think together about the vision that guides that school system's course of study. Because I, too, am a leader of a large organization, I am aware that leadership involves gathering the community and, together, finding a North Star. Someone needs to say to the extended community, "This pathway is an important one for us to follow. Come, come...."

Teachers and school leaders together, need to think about the rights of learners: "What does the Bill of Rights in the teaching of writing consist of for the learners in our care? What conditions are so essential that every child deserves these conditions, these opportunities to learn?" A system must adopt common denominators that are within reach of the people in that system and that are aligned to the system's standards.

The educators that I work closely with tend to agree that the following are the necessary foundations for the writing workshop:

We need to teach every child to write. Almost every day, every K–5 child needs between fifty and sixty minutes for writing and writing instruction.

Although I strongly believe teachers should make decisions about their own teaching, none of us can decide not to teach math, nor can a teacher say, "I teach math across every subject area," and then merely sprinkle math here and there across the day, asking children to add up the number of pages they've read or to count the minutes until school is dismissed for the day and calling that a math curriculum. Yet in some districts it is acceptable for teachers to say, "I teach writing across the curriculum" and for those teachers to then not regard writing as a subject in the school day. I regard this as a problem. Children's success in many disciplines is utterly reliant on their abilities to write; children deserve writing to be a subject that is taught and studied just like reading or math. In school systems that are affiliated with the Teachers College Reading and Writing Project, it is nonnegotiable that every child spends time every day learning to write, that there is a planned curriculum for that time, and that during that time, the teacher is teaching writing.

It is also necessary that during that time, children actually write and do so for long stretches of time. Writing is a skill, like playing the trumpet or swimming or playing tennis or reading. There is very little a teacher can do from the front of the room that will help a learner become skilled at playing an instrument or swimming or playing tennis or reading—and writing is no different. Skills are learned through practice. As my sons' tennis teacher says, "Success in tennis has an awful lot to do with the number of balls hit." Similarly, success in reading directly correlates with the number of hours spent reading. John Guthrie's recent study illustrates that fourth graders who read at the second-grade level spend a half hour a day reading and fourth graders who read at the eighth-grade level spend four hours a day reading.[1] Similarly, success in writing directly relates to the amount of writing and rewriting a person does.

This means that day after day, children need to write. They need to write for long stretches of time—for something like forty minutes of each day's writing workshop—and they need to write for almost the same length of time at home most evenings.

Volume and stamina matter. It is almost impossible for a child to write well if that child doesn't write fluently, because writing well involves elaboration. (This is true enough that a recent study by an MIT professor found that a student's score on the writing component of the SAT correlated almost exactly with the length of the student's essay![2]) Because volume matters, many teachers help students set incremental goals for themselves. At first, the goal might be to write a half page within one writing workshop, but within a few months, the goal can be a page or a page and a half of in-school writing each day, and soon, a similar amount

of at-home writing. Students date each day's writing, and all writing stays in the students' notebooks and folders until the unit of study culminates in a publishing party. This means that teachers, literacy coaches, and principals can look through students' writing folders and notebooks and see the work that any student produced on Monday, Tuesday, Wednesday, and so forth. Of course, there may be a day when writers devote their writing time to a study of exemplar texts or to an especially long discussion about writing rough drafts. But those days are exceptions. Writers write, and a wonderful thing about writing is that it is immediately visible. This allows a school system to hold itself accountable for ensuring that every child has the opportunity and the responsibility to write every day.

We need to teach children to write texts like other writers write—memoirs, stories, editorials, essays, poems—for an audience of readers, not just for the teacher.

Donald Murray, the Pulitzer Prize–winning writer who is widely regarded as the father of writing process, recalls the piano lessons he was given as a child. The school system announced that anyone wanting to learn to play the piano should report to the cafeteria after school. Murray recalls his palpable excitement: at last, he was going to learn to make those beautiful melodies! In the cafeteria, children sat in rows, facing the front. Each child was given a cardboard keyboard and shown how to lay his or her hands on it so as to "play" notes. Children pressed their cardboard keyboards, but there was no music, no melody. Murray left and never returned.

Children deserve opportunities to write real writing; this means that instead of writing merely "compositions" and "reports," children need to

---

[1] "Engaging Young Readers: Promoting Achievement and Motivation." *Solving Problems in the Teaching of Literacy.* Guilford Publications, 2000.

[2] "SAT Essay Test Rewards Length and Ignores Errors" by Michael Winerip, *The New York Times,* May 4, 2005, article cites MIT Professor Les Perelman's research on SAT.

write in all the genres that exist in the world. A child should know that he or she is writing something—a poem, an essay, a book review, a lab report, a short story—that writers write and readers read.

Children not only deserve daily opportunities to write particular kinds of things—to write *something* that exists in the world—they also deserve opportunities to write for *someone*—for readers who will respond to what they have written. Children deserve to write knowing that their final pieces of writing—the ones writers produce after planning and drafting and revising—stand a good chance of being read by readers. Otherwise how will young writers learn that writing well involves aiming to create an effect? Craft and deliberate choice in writing are the result of thinking, as we write, "This will surprise them! They'll sit up and take notice right here," or "This will be a funny part," or "If I can pull this section off, I think it will give my readers goosebumps." In order to write with this sense of agency, students deserve opportunities to see readers' responses to their writing. They need these opportunities midway through their work with a text, and they also need their final pieces to reach responsive readers.

Giving children opportunities to write *something*—a memoir, a poem—for *someone*—a friend, a grandfather—makes it likely that writing will engage children and that they will feel as if the work they are doing is real, credible, and substantial. Children should not be asked to learn to play music on cardboard keyboards or to learn to write on ditto sheets.

Writers do not write with words and convention alone; writers write above all with meaning. Children will invest themselves more in their writing if they are allowed— indeed, if they are taught—to select their own topics and to write about subjects that are important to them.

Try this. Pick up a pen and write a few sentences about the sequence of actions you did just before picking up this book. Do it on paper or in your mind.

Now pause and try something different. Think about a moment in your life that for some reason really affected you. It might be the tiniest of moments, but it gave you a lump in your throat, it made your heart skip. The last time you saw someone. The time you realized you could actually do that thing you'd been longing to do. The encounter with that special person. Write (or mentally think through) the story of that indelible moment. On the page (or just in your mind's eye) try to capture the essence of that bit of life.

You will find that doing the one kind of writing—in which you throw out any old words —and doing the other kind of writing—in which you reach for the precise words that will capture something dear to you—are utterly different. In order for children to learn to write and to grow as writers, it is absolutely essential that they are invested in their writing and that they care about writing well. Children (indeed, all of us) are far more apt to be invested in writing if we are writing something real and meaningful and if we are writing for real, responsive readers.

It is hard to imagine an argument against letting children choose their own topics for most of the writing they do. Although the craft, strategies, and qualities of good writing and the processes of writing vary somewhat depending on whether someone is writing an essay or a poem (and therefore there are advantages to the teacher's suggesting that the whole community work for a time within a shared genre), good writing does not vary based on whether it's about the day Grandfather died or the first moments in a new school. Teachers can gather the entire class together and teach them anything—the importance of detail or strategies for making simple sentences more complex—knowing the instruction will be equally relevant to children who are engaged in writing about a wide array of different subjects.

The easiest way to help children love writing is to invite them to write about subjects they care about. When children have the opportunity and responsibility to choose their own subjects, they are not only much more apt to be invested in their writing, they are also much more apt to be knowledgeable about their topics. In addition, they can learn what it means to rediscover subjects through the process of writing about them.

Obviously, there may be some instances when you decide to ask the entire class to write on a shared topic; when there are compelling reasons to ask this of children, this other value will trump the value of topic choice.

Children deserve to be explicitly taught the skills and strategies of effective writing, and the qualities of good writing. This teaching will be dramatically more powerful if teachers are studying the teaching of writing and if they are responsive to what students are doing and trying to do as writers. Children also deserve a teacher who demonstrates a commitment to writing.

Although it is important for children to write every day, it is not enough for them simply to have the opportunity to write. Children also deserve instruction. They are extremely vulnerable to instruction. I can walk into a classroom, look over children's writing, and know immediately whether children are being taught to write well, because strong, clear instruction dramatically affects student writing.

It is not enough for we teachers to turn down the lights, turn on the music, and say, "Write." It is not enough for children to have time each day to crank out genre-less, audience-less, model-less, revision-less journal entries. Instead, we need to teach explicitly the qualities, habits, and strategies of effective writing; moreover, we need to assess the results of our teaching in order to ensure that every child has learned what we have taught. Most strategies and qualities of good writing are multileveled. Every child in every classroom can learn to write narratives that are chronologically ordered and detailed. Every child can learn to include direct quotations. Some children will spell better than others, some will use more complex sentence structures than others, but many of the skills and strategies of skilled writing are within reach of every writer.

Children not only deserve to be instructed in writing well, they also deserve to learn from a teacher who is well informed about the qualities, processes, and habits of skilled writing. This is most apt to happen if teachers participate in professional development on the teaching of writing and if teachers across grade levels plan teaching together, capitalizing on any teachers within the group who have invested time studying the teaching of writing and/or working on their own writing. Teachers' collaborative study in the teaching of writing will take on heart and soul, nuance and fire, when we ourselves try the techniques we ask children to try, writing our own personal narratives, essays, poems, and memoirs.

The quality of writing instruction will rise dramatically not only when we study the teaching of writing but also when we study our own children's intentions and progress as writers. Strong writing instruction is always tailored for and responsive to the writer. A writing teacher functions above all as a coach, watching from the sidelines as writers go through the process of writing, then intervening to help one individual after another see what she is doing that is or isn't working, ways in which she can work with more skill. The teaching of writing is always about helping individuals, small groups, and classes as a whole ratchet their work up a notch.

As important as it is for children to learn *how* to write well, it is equally important for them to learn to *care* about writing. It is enormously important that we, as teachers, demonstrate and expect a love of writing.

We need to provide children the opportunity and instruction necessary for them to cycle through the writing process regularly as they write, rehearse, draft, revise, edit, and publish their writing.

The scientific method is widely regarded as so fundamental to science that children use it whether they are studying sinking and floating in kindergarten or friction and inertia in high school. Likewise, the writing process is fundamental to all writing; therefore it is important that children of every age receive frequent opportunities to rehearse, draft, revise, and edit their writing. If a child is going to write an editorial, his first concern should probably not be, "How do I write the first sentence?" but rather, "What are the qualities of great editorials? What does the writing life look like for an editorial writer? What sorts of entries does an editorial writer collect in his or her notebook?"

Most of the time, children should be expected to proceed through the writing process. This means that, most of the time, they should anticipate and have opportunities to plan for and rehearse writing. They should usually write tentatively at first, producing at least a portion of a rough draft (or two). They should certainly have the opportunity to reread a rough draft, viewing it through a variety of lenses, including "What am I really trying to say here? How can I bring forth that meaning?" and "What sense will a reader make of this? How can I make my meaning clearer and more compelling for my reader?" A writer will always write with the conventions that are easily under his control, but once a text is almost ready for readers, the writer will want to edit it, taking extra care to make the text clear, forceful, and correct. Often the writer will use outside assistance—from dictionaries, peers, a teacher—in order to increase the level of clarity and correctness in a text.

Writers read. Writers read texts of all sorts, and we read as insiders, aiming to learn specific strategies for writing well.

Any effective writing curriculum acknowledges that it is important for writers to be immersed in wonderful literature. Children will not learn to write well if they are not immersed in and affected by texts that other authors have written. They need the sounds and power of good literature to be in their bones. They need a felt sense for how effective stories can go, for the way in which a poem can make a reader gasp and be still. They also need some opportunities to study closely a few texts that are similar to those they are trying to make.

Children especially need opportunities to read-as-writers. Imagine that you were asked to write a foreword for this book. My hunch is that you'd do exactly as I did when Georgia Heard asked me to write my first foreword ever. I pulled books from my shelf, and searched for forewords. I found half a dozen, and read them ravenously. "How does a foreword really go?" I asked. Children, too, deserve the chance to read like writers.

By studying the work of other authors, students not only develop a felt sense of what it is they are trying to make but they also learn the traditions of that particular kind of text. Poets leave white space, essayists advance ideas, storytellers convey the passage of time. All writers care that the sound of our words matches the tone of our meaning, all writers care that we choose precisely right words. By studying texts that resemble those they are trying to make, children learn the tools of their trade.

CHAPTER 3

THE WRITING PROCESS FOR UPPER-ELEMENTARY-GRADE WRITERS

When I was a fourth grader, my teacher taught writing by assigning us topics and page lengths. We wrote at home, bringing our completed stories, essays, poems, and reports to school a few days after they were assigned. After a bit, we'd receive the papers back, each with a grade for content, a grade for mechanics, and a few marginal comments. I expect many of us were "taught" writing that way. That was before the Writing Revolution.

Approximately two decades ago, a flurry of books and articles called for and created a Writing Revolution. Peter Elbow, Donald Murray, James Moffett, Ken Macrorie, and a series of edited volumes titled *Writers at Work* combined to popularize the message that when writers write, we do not sit down with a quill pen and immediately produce graceful, compelling prose. Instead writers work through a process of writing, a process that contains recursive "stages." Different people use different terms when describing those stages. For example, some use the term *prewriting* and some *rehearsal*, but either way, widespread agreement has emerged that writers spend time preparing for writing. This stage involves living "writerly lives," collecting material for writing, jotting alternative plans for how a piece of writing might go, talking about one's topic, and reading texts that resemble the text one hopes to write. Writers also *draft*. Early drafts are more like playing in clay than inscribing in marble; a writer might try alternative leads, explore different voices for a text, or free write, keeping her eyes glued on the subject and trying to capture the contours of it in tentative form. Writers shift back and forth between drafting and revising. *Revision* means, quite literally, to see again. During revision, a writer pulls back from a draft in order to reread and rethink, "What is it I really want to say?" Writers revise in order to discover and convey meaning. Revision may involve rewriting a lead, re-angling a story, elaborating on important sections, and deleting unimportant ones. It usually involves anticipating a reader's response: "What do I want my reader to feel? To know?" Revision may or may not involve a second or third draft. Finally, writers *edit,* which involves correcting, smoothing out, linking, clarifying. During editing, writers think about spelling, punctuation, and word choice, yes, but writers also think about language and clarity.

The news that professional writers go through a process of writing was accompanied by the equally important news that even young children can experience the writing process. More than two decades ago, a team of us from the University of New Hampshire—Donald Graves, Susan Sowers, and I, followed by many others—wrote articles and books showing that children, too, can rehearse, draft, revise, and edit their writing and suggesting that when we observe and coach young writers in their process of writing, their growth in writing can be spectacular. The research on young children and the writing process was the talk of the town in the eighties. Since then, the idea that educators need to teach the writing process has become so widely accepted that this is almost a mainstream premise. Many standardized tests even include planning pages and remind writers to leave time to revise and edit their essays. Most language arts textbooks have incorporated the terms (if not the real concepts) of the writing process into their curriculum. And in New York City, for example, every elementary school teacher is now expected to lead a writing workshop in which all students work their way through the writing process.

TEACHING EIGHT-, NINE- AND TEN-YEAR-OLDS THE WRITING PROCESS

Although the rhetoric behind the idea of teaching writing process involves talk like this—"Children should be invited to write like real writers"—the truth is that children can only approximate the processes that adult writers use. An eight-year-old will not write exactly like Robert Frost or Patricia Polacco, nor do adult writers all write exactly like one another! Even when a school system has adopted a writing process approach to teaching writing, teachers are still left with the job of thinking through the process that we plan to teach.

Some teachers decide to encourage each child to devise his or her own individual writing process. On any one day in these classrooms, one child will write leads to a story, another will begin and complete an all-about book, yet another will write several poems. Day after day, children in these classrooms cycle through the writing process in their own way and at their own pace. In a month, one child in a class may have written one very long rough draft, another will have worked two pieces through a series of revisions, still another will have produced a dozen lightly revised texts. Teachers in these classrooms also place a priority on each child choosing his or her genre and topic. The teachers, meanwhile, look for teachable moments in which they can extend what children do as writers.

Other teachers—and my colleagues and I fall into this category—imagine that at the start of a school year we will scaffold a class of children to progress through a version of the writing process in a roughly synchronized fashion, with some children moving more quickly and others more slowly along the same general path. Because children are traveling roughly in sync, the teacher can do a lot of explicit teaching. As the year unrolls (and as one year follows the next) the teacher provides scaffolds that support larger, more encompassing steps, giving children progressively more independence. For example, at the start of a school year, working with children who are new to the writing process, the teacher might teach one rehearsal strategy, asking all children to use that one strategy to generate ideas for that day's writing. A few days later, the same teacher might review three optional strategies for rehearsal, demonstrate a fourth, and suggest that each child select from this repertoire the one that works best for her that day. Two months later, this teacher might begin yet another narrative unit by saying, "You already know a lot of strategies for generating narrative writing, and I hope you'll again draw from that repertoire of strategies. But *this* time, I want to help you think about using those strategies to generate writing that feels more significant to you and to your readers."

Because my colleagues and I want to move upper-elementary-level children through a somewhat shared process of writing, we approach our teaching by asking, "Given that there is no *one* way to approach the challenge of writing a piece, what sequence of living, writing, and thinking feels close enough to what real writers do that we could imagine championing this approach within our writing workshops?" Of course, when we think about the process of writing that we will demonstrate for children, we also need to ask, "What will be doable (as well as worth doing) for all my children?" and "How will different children tailor this process differently in keeping with their specific hopes, passions, skills, and temperaments?"

Pacing and Materials

When trying to decide what is within children's reach, teachers need to invite not only upper-elementary students but also their younger brothers and sisters to approximate the writing process. In the schools I know best, children in the primary grades usually cycle fairly quickly through the entire writing process, producing several texts each week. Five-, six-, and seven-year-olds rehearse for writing simply by thinking of a topic, telling a partner what they will write, selecting paper with an eye toward how the text will go, drawing a sketch on each page, and saying or thinking the words that they will write on that page. Then children draft. They reread, fixing up obvious problems on their own. Otherwise, revision is usually prompted by conferences or minilessons which steer them towards particular alterations. At this age, it is easier for children to write many pieces of writing rather than linger on a single piece.

By third grade children can definitely work a bit longer and more deeply on a given piece of writing, but I do not think that in September most third graders yet have the skills or the temperament to invest a full month in working toward a single publishable piece of writing. At the start of the year, the third graders I know best cycle through the writing process at a good clip. Within a month they produce many narrative

notebook entries, develop and revise two of these, and select one of those narratives for further revision, editing, and publishing. As they become more experienced and develop a deeper knowledge of good writing and a bigger repertoire of strategies for rehearsing and revising writing, they cycle through the writing process more slowly. In this series, the first unit, *Launching the Writing Workshop*, supports children as they produce two pieces in a month, and the second unit, *Improving the Quality of Personal Narrative Writing*, supports children as they produce just one, more carefully written text in a month. However, you will adjust this rate of work to suit your own class, bearing in mind that as children become more experienced and skilled, they can work longer (not less long, as some might suppose) on any given writing project.

Third graders, like their younger counterparts, find it supportive to write on paper that physically embodies the expectations for a particular genre. In K–2 classrooms, children write narratives in small booklets, with each page carrying the story of the next thing that happened. Teachers in the primary grades make paper for children, leaving space on each page for a picture as well as for sentences. When the time comes for third graders to write a "stretched-out," detailed narrative about a small moment in their lives, many teachers suggest they do so in a grown-up version of the booklets one finds in primary classrooms. The third graders' booklets do not have spaces for drawing, but children are expected to put a dot from their timeline (and the sentence accompanying that dot) at the top of a page, and this functions much as the picture does for younger children. By third grade, teachers rarely make paper for these booklets, instead suggesting that children who are writing narratives draft on pieces of notebook paper, folded in half. If the school doesn't suffer a shortage of paper, it's ideal to put two such sheets of paper together to form a booklet, with children writing only on one side of each "page," leaving them flexibility to cut the pages apart in order to extend any one portion of a draft. Similarly, when third graders write essays, teachers suggest that children use a clean sheet of paper for each new paragraph of the essay, writing topic sentences at the tops of pages and then elaborating on them in the space below. By the time children are in fifth grade, it may be less important for the paper on which they write to physically support elaboration.

Rehearsal for Writing

The first stage of the writing process is often called "rehearsal," or "gathering entries." Children who have been in strong writing workshops during the primary grades will enter third or fourth grade able to gather and generate ideas for writing. Other children, however, are apt to sit over blank pages saying, "Nothing happens in my life," or "I don't have anything to say." In these instances, supporting rehearsal for writing means helping children learn strategies for generating whatever kind of writing they aim to write.

Although I did not always believe this, I'm now convinced that those strategies will be somewhat different depending on whether a child is writing a personal narrative, a literary essay, or a poem. For example, when teaching children to write personal narrative entries, I might suggest they take a minute to think of a person (or place or thing) that matters to them and then to list several times when they did something with that person (in that place, with that thing). Then I suggest they reread that little list, select one episode that they remember with crystal clarity, and begin to write the story of that one episode. When teaching children to write essays about literature, I might teach them to read with a set of questions in mind: "What is this text really about? What line or passage in this text captures what the author is really trying to convey?"

With a bit of instruction, children can quickly develop a small repertoire of strategies for generating writing in their genre of choice and learn to draw on their developing repertoire of strategies in order to generate writing within that genre. More than this, children learn that when they live their lives as writers, the details of their lives and of their thinking are worth writing about. They'll find themselves living with a writer's consciousness, thinking often, "I should write about this."

In upper-grade writing workshops, after teaching children a few strategies for generating writing, we encourage children to collect entries in their writer's notebooks. Ideally, we hope children will carry those notebooks (literally and figuratively) through their lives. Although it is fairly easy to teach children a few strategies for generating ideas for writing, it is less easy and more important to take the additional step and teach children to live with this perspective of being a writer, seeing potential stories, essays, and poems everywhere and thinking often, "I should jot this down. I may want to make something of it."

As soon as possible, we encourage children to carry notebooks between home and school, generating entries in both places. This doubles the volume of writing that children produce, and it also makes it much more likely that children will live their lives with the writerly consciousness of "I am one who writes," seeing their lives as full of raw material for writing. This is a very deep, important aspect of rehearsal for writing.

Teachers who are not able to rally children to write entries at home can still see growth in children's abilities to rehearse. In time, children come to the writing workshop already knowing what they want to write, which suggests that children are seeing their lives as full of stories to tell, ideas to share.

Rehearsal involves not only living like a writer and seeing potential stories and essays everywhere but also selecting from all these possibilities one seed idea that is worth developing and beginning to plan a first draft. As children become more experienced, they learn that writers select one seed idea over another because they have a sense that the chosen seed has more significance. Writers write, wanting to convey a meaning that matters. Writers think, talk, and write in order to come to an understanding of what it is we want to say.

As children become more experienced and skilled as writers, everything they learn through revision can move forward into the rehearsal stage of their writing. For example, some writers begin the year writing about gigantic topics—"my trip to my grandma's house." Only during revision do these children reread their writing and think, "Which *particular aspect* of my visit do I want to address?" With experience, however, these same children will soon learn to generate ideas for writing and to immediately screen those ideas, asking, "Will this story (essay) be focused enough?"

Similarly, the initial entries children write in their notebooks will not be detailed, written in paragraphs, and so forth. As children learn more and more, however, the work they do during rehearsal will incorporate features they earlier learned only through revision. These might include paragraphing, writing with details, showing rather than telling, developing the heart of the story, or a host of other skills. In other words, the more skilled and experienced a writer becomes, the more that writer can do during rehearsal.

A professional writer might delay drafting for six months or a year, using this time to write and critique a whole sequence of different plans for a text! Such a writer would prefer progressing through multiple *outlines* rather than multiple *drafts*. A nine-year-old child, of course, will not find it easy to scrawl a few words onto the page and then look at this outline or plan, imagining from the abbreviated notes the larger text and imagining also the problems such a text would encounter—let alone imagining another way in which that text could have been written.

Still, nine-year-olds can live like writers, seeing potential for stories and essays everywhere. They can use all they know about good writing (or good narratives, good essays, and so on) to lift the level of their entries, thus giving them taller shoulders to stand on when they select one entry to develop into a major piece of writing. These children can also learn to talk through the writing they plan to do, trying out one way and then another of approaching their subject, observing their audiences' responses to those "in-the-air" drafts and revising the drafts before they've even written a word.

Finally, upper-elementary students can learn to make simple outlines, revising these in preparation for writing. More specifically, children who are writing narratives use timelines or story mountains to plan and, more importantly, to revise the scope and sequence of an

eventual draft. They can look at a timeline of a story and think, "I should start later in the progression, closer to the action," and they can look at a story mountain and think, "I need to really build up this part of my story, it is my rising action. I need to show how he tried, tried, tried." When children write expository texts, they can outline their main idea and their supporting ideas, adjusting these to be sure their supporting ideas are parallel to one another. They can conduct research as a way to gather information to support their ideas. They can gather a variety of supporting information and make sure that their supporting information is aligned with their ideas. All of this can be done in preparation for writing a draft.

Drafting

While rehearsal and revision both involve the deliberate use of one strategy or another, drafting is less strategic. After all the work of collecting and choosing among entries, planning how the piece will go, choosing paper and imagining the piece laid out on the page, telling the story or teaching the information to another person in order to develop a voice with which to convey the material, the writer takes pen in hand and writes.

I often teach children that narrative writers first try different leads, choosing between them. I expect that children who are writing narratives will try replaying a small action or recording a bit of dialogue. I expect that children will try starting the story at various places in the sequence of events, experimenting with a narrower and broader focus. As children try different leads, I give myself a bit of time to move among them, working toward what for me is a very important goal: when a child writes a narrative, I hope that the child will envision what happened in his or her mind's eye and write the story, fast and long.

Peter Elbow, the great writing teacher and author of *Writing with Power*, advises, "Don't *describe* the tree. *See* the tree!" Powerful writing does not come from thinking about penmanship, word choice, complex sentences, showing-not-telling as one writes. Powerful writing comes from being full of one's subject and keeping one's eye on that subject.

The felt sense of writing an essay is, I believe, very different from the felt sense of writing a narrative. Sometimes when we write essays, we are essentially teaching or persuading readers. The essayist assumes a teaching/explaining/persuading voice, feels full of his or her subject, and then puts pen to page, trying to write in ways that convey an idea to anticipated readers. The essayist sometimes literally copies material that she or he has gathered and sometimes leaves gaps in the draft that she or he will puzzle through later. For the essayist, as for the narrative writer, drafting is tentative, done in the spirit of exploration.

There is no question that as children grow older and more experienced, the drafts of any one piece of writing will stand on the shoulders of previous writing and especially of previous revisions. If Roy's first draft of a personal narrative in September conveyed what the characters said to each other but was only a sound track, without any mention of actions and settings to contextualize the dialogue, and if Roy worked arduously to revise that draft by adding a backdrop to the dialogue, then one would expect that in October, when he makes new narrative notebook entries and especially when he writes another first draft of a personal narrative, this time he will, from the start, intersperse dialogue with sentences conveying action and setting.

Revision

Revision means, quite literally, to *resee*. Writing is a powerful tool for thought precisely because when we write, we can put our first thoughts on the page and then take those thoughts and put them in our pocket or file and take those thoughts out another day. We can then reread and rethink our first thoughts.

As writers we learn, over time, a variety of lenses we can use to re-see and reconsider our first drafts. For starters, we shift to become readers of our own writing; we pretend we are strangers, encountering the text for the first time. We read thinking, "What will a reader make of this?" We ask, "Are there sections that are unclear? That rely on more explicit information? That are misleading? Contradictory?" Then we revise our writing so that readers will be able to make sense of what we've said.

We can also reread in order to consider our own texts in the light of our aspirations, asking, "Can I see the quality of writing that I'm aiming to achieve in this text?" In other words, if a writer has studied effective essays and learned that essays often shift between precise examples and overarching ideas, the writer might look at her own essay asking, "Does my essay shift between the general and the specific?"

Writers can, more generally, reread our own writing asking, "What works here that I can build upon?" and "What doesn't work here that I can repair or eliminate?"

The most sophisticated and important sort of revision isn't fixing up one's text so that it works more effectively to convey one's meaning. Instead, the most sophisticated sorts of revisions involve the writer looking through his draft in order to come to a deeper, more nuanced, more thoughtful understanding of the writer's content. This sort of revision begins with the writer asking, "What am I trying to say?" and then revising to highlight that meaning. In time, this sort of revision becomes more exploratory. Writers venture into unexplored terrain and stumble upon new insights that illuminate a topic not only for the reader but also for the writer.

Writers sometimes write without knowing exactly what it is we want to say; then we turn around and read our writing to learn "What is it that I think?" and "What surprises me, astonishes me, makes me catch my breath?"

Between kindergarten and fifth grade, children's abilities to revise become more sophisticated. Kindergartners revise the first day of school, but those earliest revisions typically only involve adding more details onto their drawings. In time, kindergartners will add more pages to a story, more labels or sentences to a page. By first and second grade (although with some students this happens at the end of kindergarten) children will tape flaps onto edges of a draft and use those flaps to insert details and direct quotes and elaborating information. They will sometimes write new leads or endings, taping them on top of the earlier versions. They may re-sequence pages. They will certainly rewrite key pages in order to include more detail, show-not-tell their feelings, answer reader's questions, and so forth.

Revision for upper-elementary students begins much earlier in the writing process. By the time children are eight (especially if they have grown up participating in writing workshops), revision begins right when they select a topic from a list of possibilities. They'll draft a timeline if the writing will be a narrative or a very sketchy, informal outline (boxes and bullets) if the writing will be an essay and use these graphic organizers to help them anticipate difficulties and imagine other possibilities for how their planned entry might go. Once children are in third grade, they learn to begin revising very early in the process of writing, and they use revision as a way to bring their growing knowledge of good writing to bear on what they do.

Similarly, when upper-elementary students draft and revise leads, they are doing so not only with an eye toward a good lead but also because they recognize that each lead represents a different way the text could go: "If I start it this way, it'll take too long to get to the main part."

Revision happens earlier in grades three through five because whatever strategies children use as they write one text eventually move earlier in the writing process: postwriting revision eventually becomes part of their rehearsal. For example, at first children will write a narrative and then revise it by thinking, "What is the heart of this story?" and elaborating on that one section. In time, children will plan their narratives from the start with an eye toward concentrating on the heart of their story. As they draft, they'll be thinking, "I need to build up this part. I gotta make it more intense here."

Similarly, at first children will collect a great deal of supporting material for their essays, then they'll reread and reconsider it, eliminating the many passages that don't support their point. As they become more experienced, however, these same children pause as they're making their notes to ask, "How can I angle this material so that it makes my point?"

As children's revision work begins to occur earlier in the process and as children are able to do more and more during rehearsal, the amount of time that lapses between the day the child settles on a "seed idea" (the entry the child commits to turning into a final piece of writing) and the day the child begins to write his or her first draft will grow longer. This portion of a child's writing process also varies based on the kind of text the child is writing, with fiction and essays requiring more rehearsal. I find that at the start of third grade, when these youngsters are writing personal narratives, not much productive revision work happens in the abstract. I suggest these children try a few leads and that they draft and revise a timeline, but beyond that, they need to write a draft so they can then roll up their sleeves and begin a concrete form of revision. Once children are in fifth grade, if they are experienced with the writing process, they will be able to do much more productive work as they rehearse their narratives. For example, if they are writing personal narratives, fifth graders can ask themselves (and muse over in writing) questions such as: "What will this story *really* be about?" "What will I try to show about myself in this story?" "How will this story change the way readers feel?"

Editing

Professional writers tend to postpone editing until the text is ready to be published. Like adult writers, children learn the value of writing rough drafts quickly, without pausing to use *Roget's Thesaurus* or even a dictionary in the midst of drafting. And like adult writers, children do not pore over a draft, worrying that every convention is correct, until it is time for the writing to be published.

Once the main structure and content of a draft has been revised so that the text now feels stable, writers begin to reread, checking each sentence, word, and letter from a "when you falter, alter" perspective. In our writing workshops, we teach students to read each draft successive times, each time with a new lens. Among other things, the child will read for spelling. If the child senses that a word is misspelled, she circles that word and then tries it again in the margin. In order to do this, the child needs to look at the approximate spelling, asking, "Is this partly right?" and then copy that part of the word. The child also needs to ask, "What other words do I know that might be spelled like this one?" and to use the words the child can spell to help spell unknown words. Children are encouraged to use resources to help them, including a dictionary and each other.

Editing involves much more than correcting spelling, and children are taught to check that they've included end punctuation, that their verb tenses agree, that they use a variety of punctuation and sentence structure, that their words are precise, that their pronoun references are clear. "Does this sound right?" a writer asks. "Is this exactly true? Are the words precisely chosen? Will the punctuation give readers the road signs they need?"

Teachers teach editing within minilessons, and also within mid-workshop teaching points, share sessions, and homework assignments. Obviously, teachers will tailor their lessons so they are roughly aligned with what most of the class needs, using small group instruction to provide special support for children who need it. As the year unfolds, the classroom's editing checklist will grow, with children having access to a growing list of skills. That is, in September, teachers may expect children to edit their writing looking for high-frequency words which are on the class word wall, for end punctuation and for paragraphing. By May, children will check that their pronoun references are clear, and their sentences structures, varied.

Once children have been taught to edit with particular concerns in

mind, then those skills and strategies need to move forward in the writing process, becoming part of the writer's repertoire of skills that he draws upon while scrawling a rough draft. That is, although children are not expected to fret about writing perfectly correct drafts, it is also not helpful for them to postpone all thought of spelling and punctuation until the final throes of work on a manuscript. Over time, they need to write very fast rough drafts with roughly correct spelling and punctuation. It is also important that they learn to spell a growing bank of words (and syllables) automatically. And punctuation cannot be an afterthought, inserted into a manuscript just before it goes to press! So we, as teachers, help children take a few minutes as they write their rough drafts to make sure that the conventions they "almost know" are under control. Then, during editing, children can reexamine conventions that pose problems for them, relying on resources and one another to edit these problematic areas.

Once a child has edited her own writing, a teacher will need to confer with the child, teaching the writer another few strategies she can use to edit the text. Perhaps the child will have added quotation marks correctly, but will not yet have mastered the punctuation that is expected with quotations. In the editing conference, we would support the child's use of quotation marks, and show her the next step toward correct handling of quotations. We'd go over one quote with the child, and then ask her to read through the draft, fixing the others. Meanwhile, however, there will also be some incorrect spellings and some problems with verb tenses, and we might choose not to tackle those as well. That is, in editing conferences like in every other kind of conference, a teacher makes a choice, teaching the child one or two things which seem to be within the child's reach.

Meanwhile, before the child's work is published, many teachers go through the final draft as a copy editor would, correcting on it. The child then recopies the piece, correcting most (but rarely all) of the errors. This final step calls for a decision. If teachers correct the child's final work before children recopy it, then that text will be easier for others to read. On the other hand, if teachers do this, then the child's final work does not really show what the child can do with independence, and it will be harder for us to hold ourselves to being sure that children are growing in their abilities to correct their own writing. It is important, therefore, that the next-to-final draft is kept in the child's portfolio.

Cycling Through the Entire Process

Just as children need to have a felt sense of how a narrative or an essay tends to go, they need to have a felt sense of how the process of writing that kind of text is apt to go. For example, we don't want the stage of gathering entries to be so long that children can't feel that it is just a prelude to selecting one seed idea to develop. The gathering of entries can't feel like an end in itself—the stage of using those entries has to follow directly upon it, within a short enough time frame that kids recognize the reasons they collected those entries. I want children to plan and draft their writing anticipating the day they'll revise it and, better yet, anticipating the day they'll send the text out into the world. When I am creating a version of the writing process for a class, I look for indications that the version of the writing process that I imagine for them matches what they can do with only a little support. I want to see that children are productive, engaged, and purposeful throughout the entire process.

CHAPTER 4

PLANNING A YEARLONG CURRICULUM

For more than two decades, writing workshops have been characterized by their structure. Workshops usually begin with explicit instruction delivered in a minilesson, followed by a long stretch of time in which students work with some independence on projects of great importance to them while the teacher circulates, conferring and sometimes leading small groups to lift the level of writing-in-progress and to teach students skills and strategies they can also bring to future pieces of writing. Workshops tend to end with some form of share, either among the whole group or between partners or members of response groups.

THE ARGUMENT FOR TEACHERS TO COLLABORATIVELY DESIGN SHARED CURRICULAR CALENDARS

One of the greatest contributions that the Teachers College Reading and Writing Project has made to this widely shared image of a writing workshop is the notion that workshops are characterized not only by these ongoing structures but also by changing units of study. Thirty years ago, when I wrote the first edition of *The Art of Teaching Writing*, I imagined that each class of children would probably progress through their own unique sequence of units of study. At that time, I imagined that some units might last three weeks, others six weeks, and that as one unit came to an end, the teacher and children would together envision a new unit of study, embarking on that upcoming inquiry when the time was right.

Since then, my ideas on a yearlong curriculum have become less informal and spontaneous and more planned and collaborative. Now, in most New York City elementary schools and in thousands of other schools, teachers across a grade level spend a full day or an afternoon in May or June thinking together about the units of study for their upcoming year's writing workshop. In general, teachers assume that all the classrooms at a particular grade level will move roughly in sync through a preplanned, collaboratively chosen sequence of month-long units of study. A letter containing an overview of the yearlong writing curriculum goes home to parents early in the school year.

There are, of course, lots of exceptions. For example, sometimes cohorts of teachers decide that the length of units will vary. One unit will be only three weeks long, another will take six weeks. Sometimes not all teachers and classrooms on a grade level join in on the shared curriculum—instead, a "friendship group" of several teachers across different grade levels embraces this chance to teach within a community of practice. Sometimes teachers agree to travel in sync for most of the year but also set aside a month or two to go their own ways.

But on the whole we find that when all the teachers across a grade level in a school agree to plan and teach in alignment with one another, this relatively simple decision can do more to improve the professional learning lives at the school than almost any other decision teachers and school leaders could possibly make. And few things matter more than the professional learning lives of the people who live and work together in a school.

Roland Barth, author of *Improving Schools from Within*, points out that all too often, relationships among teachers are like relationships among two-year-olds playing next to one another in a sandbox. When teachers engage in this "parallel play," we do not share our "toys"; one teacher has the teaching equivalent of a shovel, another, a pail. Not only that, we also do not talk to one another. We *do* talk, all the time,

but never to one another, and we would never think of combining efforts to make a shared "castle." Other times relationships among teachers can be hostile, as we battle for limited resources and limited recognition. And sometimes relationships are congenial, with teachers engaging in pleasant small talk together under the shared premise illustrated by a sign in one faculty room that said "No Children Allowed in This Room" before it was revised, by a handwritten addition, to read, "No *Talking About* Children Allowed in This Room." Finally, some faculty rooms are characterized by collegiality, and Barth argues that in these schools, teachers have the greatest system of professional development imaginable. In these schools, we plan teaching together, wish one another well as teachers, observe one another's teaching, and stand on one another's shoulders in order to make our teaching as strong as possible.

When teachers adopt a shared curricular calendar for writing and make the commitment to travel in sync with one another through a collaboratively designed curriculum, there are suddenly wonderful reasons to spend prep periods planning together. Teachers write together, sharing the stories of our own lives, and we gain insights from our own experiences as writers in a community of writers. We bring one another's drafts into classrooms, helping all the children in a school see all their teachers as richly literate people. Suddenly it becomes incredibly meaningful for us to convene around student writing, poring over the work that students in various classrooms are doing in order to think together about predictable problems students encounter and possible ways to support them. Teachers who are more experienced or more able to study the teaching of writing can lend a hand to those who need help writing minilessons, locating mentor texts, and evaluating student work.

When teachers across a grade level collaborate in this way on the teaching of writing, we provide one another with important support. Decades of work in the teaching of writing have convinced me that wise methods of teaching usually do not emerge *sui generis* from a single gifted and talented teacher. Wise methods of teaching do not come from our genes alone but from our communities of practice. How important it is for schools to devise schedules so that teachers across a grade level can meet together several times a week as a support and study group, collaborating around anticipated units of study. Within these groups, teachers write together, study children's literature together, assess student writing together, and draft, revise and share minilessons and small-group strategy lessons together.

This structure also allows professional development to be aligned with instruction. A staff developer, for example, can work for a month in four schools, one day a week in each, then move and spend one day a week in a second cluster of four schools, returning during the third month to the first set of schools. While the staff developer is working in a school, she can help several grade-specific groups of teachers plan and teach their units of study. Early on, the staff developer provides demonstration teaching and coaching to support that unit of study; over time, she provides coaching and guided practice as teachers assume more and more responsibility. In time, the teachers can be teaching one unit of study to kids—say, a unit on literary essays—and the staff developer can be teaching a different unit of study to teachers—a unit on supporting reading-writing connections, or on methods of teaching that support increasing independence, or on small group work in a writing workshop.

Let me explain the way in which staff developers might work in more detail. For example, an upper-grade staff developer might work Wednesdays in September at P.S. 260, starting each day with an 8:30–9:30 "lab site" class of third graders, with all the second- and third-grade teachers participating. Later in the day, the staff developer might work similarly with all the fourth-grade teachers and then with all the fifth-grade teachers. The staff developer then leads a study-group session for each of the

three groups of teachers, helping them learn from methods of teaching they saw demonstrated and also helping them plan their teaching for the upcoming week. As the unit of study comes to a close and the staff developer prepares to leave to spend the next month with different schools, she helps each of the study groups plan for and perhaps launch the upcoming unit of study, with these groups of teachers then teaching and developing curriculum on their own. A month later, when the staff developer returns, the teachers again, in collaboration, construct a third unit of study. When teachers across a grade level share curricular calendars, it is easier to ensure that professional development directly supports classroom teaching.

THE EMPHASIS IN THIS WRITING CURRICULUM: LEARNING TO STRUCTURE TEXT

All of this starts with a group of teachers asking, "How might a yearlong curriculum in the teaching of writing go?" In order to make headway with this question, it is helpful to ask a follow-up question: "What big ideas will underlie my idea—our idea—for how this curriculum will unfold?" For example, when teachers develop a social studies curriculum, we need to decide what aspects of history are so important that they deserve to be spotlighted. Perhaps the teachers will decide to highlight the relationship between geography and culture or to celebrate the variety of cultures that come together in America. Those choices angle the work of the year and the sequence of that work. Similarly, when teachers devise a curriculum for teaching writing, we first need to ask, "What ideas will take preeminence in this curriculum?" There is no right answer to that question, and over the years I've found it exhilarating to explore several very different ways to imagine a yearlong curriculum.

This series of books grows out of the decision to highlight the importance of structure (as well as process) in the teaching of writing. I do not want to argue that there is something sacrosanct about this particular emphasis, only that it is one very worthwhile option. I came to believe that we'd do well to emphasize structure in writing after studying the written work that students were producing in writing workshops across the country. Many students were focused primarily on using writerly craft and reading–writing connections to "pretty up" their texts with fancy beginnings and endings, sound effects, sensory details, and metaphors and similes. But far too many of the pieces were structured in such hodge-podge fashion that it seemed as if the writers were worrying about door-knockers on homes that had no foundation or walls!

The written traces of kids' processes suggested the writers had written their first drafts by selecting a topic—summers at Grandma's house—and then piling on whatever loosely related material came to mind. Then it seemed the children had either asked the teacher, "Can I be done?" and been told no or had gotten a second wind; either way they'd again written whatever came to mind that was loosely related to the chosen topic, often repeating much of what they'd already said. Finally, the writers had set about revising these drafts by adding special effects—sound effects, a pretty metaphor, endings that referred to their beginnings. The resulting pieces might have some lovely sections, but the texts as wholes were often chaotic, hard to follow, and not representative of any particular genre. Studying them, I came to believe that young writers would profit from learning to approach a draft with a specific text structure in mind.

During this time, I had also been meeting periodically with literacy leaders from across the country who were hoping to revise the standards for literacy published by the National Center for Education and the Economy. My belief that structures—or kinds—of writing need to figure more preeminently in children's plans were echoed by other members of that committee, and together we posited that the texts fourth and fifth graders write can be divided into these main categories:

- Narrative texts: personal narratives, narrative memoir, short fiction, biography, narrative nonfiction
- Persuasive or expository essays
- Functional (also called procedural or how-to) texts
- Informational writing: reports, brochures, all-about books
- Poetry

In the primary grades (and especially in the series *Units of Study for Primary Writing*) children learn to do *all* these kinds of writing within the writing workshop, with the exception of the fairly advanced genre of persuasive or expository essays. By the time children are in upper-elementary grades, however, it seems to me that functional writing can take place mostly within math and science classrooms, informational writing in content area studies. (Both those claims, by the way, are debatable and could be rethought.) The writing workshop can then be dedicated to helping students write narratives texts, expository/persuasive essays, and poetry—and above all, helping them write these genres well and with enough enjoyment that children initiate this work within their own independent learning lives.

When thinking through a yearlong curriculum on writing, I generally begin with the idea that children will first write personal narratives, learning through this work about both the writing process and qualities of good narrative writing. After two months of narrative writing, it will probably be time for them to try their hand at expository writing, starting with the personal essay. After that I imagine children shuttling between narrative and expository writing. After writing essays, children benefit from returning to narrative writing, this time to write short fiction. This, in turn, nicely supports them to read short texts and write literary essays. Children also need the opportunity to write poetry.

In addition, teachers and children may plan a unit on revision or on author studies or on a particular quality of writing (such as show-don't-tell) or on another kind-of-writing (such as journalism or narrative non-fiction). If teachers want children to practice expository texts on-the-run, teachers may design a unit on Writing to Make a Difference, enabling children to write editorials and persuasive letters. Finally, before the year is over, students need to learn that writers do not always begin with a specific form in mind, pouring content into that form. Sometimes writers start with content and, as we write, consider a variety of forms (and create their own hybrid forms) for conveying their meaning. We encourage this very creative kind of writing in a unit on memoir.

There is no one "right way" for a yearlong curriculum to proceed. In this series, I lay out one curricular journey, one that is especially important to the community within which I teach. I deliberately do not include enough units to fill an entire year; later in this book, I suggest ways in which you and your colleagues can author additional units of study tailored to your children and to your own passions.

A RECOMMENDED CURRICULAR CALENDAR

September

UNIT 1: LAUNCHING THE WRITING WORKSHOP

We start the year by teaching children some of the biggest lessons they'll ever learn. First and most important, we teach them that their lives and their thoughts are worth writing about. We help children realize that the small moments of their lives can be compelling stories, and we help them feel committed to capturing the truth of their experience in words.

The first lessons in this unit center on topic choice. We teach children a number of strategies they can draw on in order to generate their own ideas for writing, and we set them free from a dependency on the teacher. Children will benefit from knowing that writers think of a person, then brainstorm moments they've spent with that person, choose one moment, and write the story. Writers similarly think of places that matter to them, brainstorm moments that occurred in those places, choose one moment, and write the story. Writers know that objects and photographs from their lives hold stories and that by listening to the stories of others, we can recall our own stories. Naomi Nye's beautiful poem "Valentine for Ernest Mann" reminds writers that "poems hide...in the shadows of our room they are hiding." Stories hide too, and with just a few minilessons we can be sure that all our students know where important stories are likely to hide.

Many teachers find that in this first unit, it helps to celebrate the fact that stories of significance can be found in the smallest and most ordinary occasions. Perhaps after children throng back into the classroom after lunch, we will want to help them choose one small story from all the many that occurred while they were eating and tell that story as well as possible to their partners. In this fashion, we can teach students to reexamine the everyday routines of their lives in search of stories that have humor, beauty, and drama.

Meanwhile, during this unit children learn the essentials of narrative writing. They learn that narratives are just that—stories. In a personal narrative, one character (presumably the writer) experiences one thing, then the next, then the next. These texts are chronologically ordered. Children also learn that their narratives will be more effective if the writer has zoomed in on a small episode, written with detail, expanded the heart of the story, made their characters talk—and above all "made a movie in the mind" and then recorded that movie on the page. As children learn to write in ways that reflect all that they have already learned about focus, detail, strong leads, and so forth, their writing will improve in very noticeable ways. The improvements in children's writing should prove to them that learning to write well matters and thus launch them into the year.

One of the few nonnegotiable qualities of narrative writing is the hard-to-describe (and hard-to-achieve) quality that some teachers refer to as "writing in the moment" or "making a movie in your mind." If a child talks "all about" an event—summarizing it with sentences like "It was a good baseball game. We won 6 to 2. I got a lot of hits."—then the child is *commenting on* the game rather than telling the story of it. The child has not yet grasped the idea of writing in a storyteller's voice. If, on the other hand, his piece begins, "I grabbed a bat and walked up to the plate. I looked at the pitcher and nodded. 'I'm ready,' I said," then the child is writing a story. Most children need to be reminded to make movies in their mind and to write so readers can picture exactly what is happening.

During this unit, many children will profit from learning a very simple form of focus. For example, a child might initially plan to write a page-long piece depicting his whole day at the beach, but because of our teaching, he'll write instead about body surfing on one wave. Another child will decide that instead of retelling the entire trip to Grandma's house, she will focus on how she accidentally let the pigs loose. As children narrow the time span of their stories, it is crucial that they then elaborate on the portion of the event that remains in their spotlight. In other words, the main reason to "zoom in" or to "write about a little seed story, not about a big watermelon topic" is that this makes it more likely that the writer will relive an episode with enough detail that the reader, too, can experience the event.

As children learn about narrative writing, some of the lessons will be explicit, taught in minilessons and conferences. But some of the lessons will be implicit, gleaned as children are immersed in texts that sound like those we hope they will soon write. It is not always easy to find published personal narratives, so we also share realistic fiction, especially picture books and short stories that resemble the stories about small moments the children will write. Even just one dearly loved and closely studied text can infuse a writing workshop with new energy.

This unit of study is designed to launch a writing workshop that is well managed enough that children can proceed with some

independence. Children learn the structures and rituals of a writing workshop. They learn to gather for a minilesson, to sit and listen throughout most of it, to "turn and talk" with a partner at the designated moment. They learn that they can get themselves started on writing, work past the hard parts, rely on one another as well as themselves, share their writing, and so forth. Soon children will be able to get themselves started writing new entries without needing any input from the teacher; this means that during one day's writing workshop they'll write one entry after another, working with independence.

During this launching unit, most children write two focused personal narrative stories and then select one for further revision, editing and publication.

October/November

UNIT 2: RAISING THE QUALITY OF PERSONAL NARRATIVE WRITING

Although this unit is titled *Raising the Quality of Personal Narrative Writing,* the real goal is to improve the quality of the writing—and of the writers—in general. We linger for another month of work in personal narrative writing, before shifting to a focus on expository writing, because we know that real progress comes not from constantly exposing children to yet another form of writing but from working long enough within one form to help children write longer, more significant, more conventional, and more graceful pieces in general.

We begin the unit by telling children they will be revisiting narrative writing and helping them understand this means they need to draw on all they already know. This is a perfect opportunity to teach children that writers carry with them and draw on a cumulative repertoire of strategies. For example, we can say, "You already have a whole repertoire of strategies for generating narrative writing," and briefly direct their attention to the charts listing strategies they learned during the earlier unit. When children begin to draft new personal narrative entries, we can ask them to look back at the piece they published (after revision and editing) at the end of the previous unit. Since they learned to write focused, sequential stories that included direct quotations, details, paragraphs, and end punctuation, we can suggest that their new entries should demonstrate all they have already learned as writers. This unit can definitely break children of the habit of regarding each day as nothing more than a time to practice that day's minilesson!

Once the unit has gotten underway with this emphasis on writers' drawing on all they already know, you will want to find important ways to lift the quality of students' work. Chances are good that the stories children wrote during the first unit of study were sequenced, detailed, and dull. One important way to lift the level of writing in this unit is to help children write stories that matter. There are many ways to help children bring out more significance in their writing. For starters, we may want to teach children strategies for generating narrative entries that stand a greater chance of having emotional weight and a story arc. In addition to drawing on the strategies they learned in the first unit, children also write narratives about the first (or last) time they did something, a time they learned something, and a time they felt a strong emotion—hope, worry, sadness. The resulting stories are often significant and shapely.

A second way to lift the level of student writing is to rally children to look really closely at the ways in which writers create texts that matter. We encourage children to read texts like those they will write, to let those texts affect them, and then to pause and ask, "What has this writer done that has affected me?"

Since we are guiding students to notice aspects of published texts that we believe will be especially important to them, this unit relies on assessment. Are children already writing focused, detailed, chronological pieces? If not, we'll want to teach the easiest way to focus personal narratives, which is to limit the time span of the story. Sometimes teachers refer to focused narratives as "small moment stories," although the technical word that writers use for this is *scenes* (as in scenes of a play, not scenery). But once children grasp what it means to write effectively about a brief episode, we can show them that narratives need not stay within the confines of a half-hour episode! Narratives actually comprise several scenes glued together with bits of exposition (or narration) between them.

In this unit we can suggest that a child look at any short story and notice that writers often put a few scenes (or small moments) one after another. This is what many people mean when they say that a story has a beginning, a middle, and an end. For example, the child who has written a small moment vignette about getting a bike for her birthday will construct a better story if she sets up the incident by first telling about an earlier time when she begged for the bike. Similarly, the child who writes about defending the goal in a hockey game will construct a more effective story if he first backs up to recreate the moment when he put on his goalie pads and worried they might not be thick enough.

Whether children are writing one episode or linking several together, we will definitely teach them that writers focus our pieces not only by narrowing the time frame in which we write but also by deciding on the angle from which to tell a story. We teach children to ask, "What am I trying to show about myself through this story? What do I want readers to know about me? How can I bring that meaning out in this episode?" We help children learn that the same story can be told differently, depending on the theme the writer wants to bring out. An episode about falling from the monkey bars could be written to show that the writer was afraid but conquered her fears or to show that peer pressure goaded the writer to take stupid risks.

In this unit, it is especially important to select a few touchstone texts for children to study. Ideally, they will be personal narratives—but sometimes teachers may choose instead a fictional story, explaining that although the text is really fiction, it is written as a narrative. I recommend the narrative about a red sweater embedded in "Eleven," by Sandra Cisneros. I also recommend selected pages from Jean Little's memoir *Little by Little*, Patricia MacLachlan's *Journey*, Gary Soto's *A Summer Life*, Amy Ehrlich's *When I Was Your Age: Original Stories About*

Growing Up, and *Chicken Soup for Kids*. Some picture books can be useful in this unit including Crews' *Shortcut*, Yolen's *Owl Moon*, Keats' *Peter's Chair* or *The Snowy Day* or Willems' *Knuffle Bunny*.

During this unit, we invite children to study narratives written by an author they admire, paying attention to what works in those texts. We help them read these texts as insiders, noticing sections that particularly affect them and then examining the text closely, thinking, "What has the author done to create this effect?" In the end, children also need to ask, "What effect do I want to create in my text and how could I create it?"

Once students have drafted, you'll teach them to revise, and this work will probably be informed by knowing how stories go. Stories have settings; have your students developed theirs? Children may also study effective leads and endings, the use of dialogue, and ways of showing the passage of time. Have they considered that stories usually contain a problem and a solution? If a child writes about the day he gets a bike, he may want to set up this vignette by telling how all his life he longed for a bike. Children can use their knowledge of good narratives to develop their writing; they also learn new strategies for generating story ideas that are apt to contain a story arc.

November/December

UNIT 3: BREATHING LIFE INTO ESSAYS

This unit of study is designed to help students with the difficult and exhilarating work of learning to write well within an expository structure. At the start of this unit, we point out that we could conceivably write about a topic—say a visit to Grandma's—as a narrative, retelling it chronologically, or as a non-narrative, or essay, advancing a certain idea (visits to Grandma's farm feel like time travel, for example). For some students, the fact that they can write about personal topics in a genre other than a personal narrative will be a new realization. The terms narrative and non-narrative or essay refer to structure and genre, not to

content. In this unit, each child will write a personal essay in which she advances a theme of personal significance, arguing, for example, that it's hard being an only child or claiming "my dog is my best friend."

A teacher could choose to hurry kids through this unit, showing them how to whip up modest yet well-structured and competent little essays. However, we argue that there are many reasons to take one's time, teaching students how to write these essays well and harvesting all the learning opportunities found along the way. If we help children write lots of rough drafts and do lots of revision with the goal of learning as much as possible about logical thought, this unit can have enormous payoffs. Then, after helping kids spend a month writing one essay, we can show students they also have the option of churning out a quick essay in a day—or even in fifteen minutes! This, of course, provides children with test preparation.

As with any unit of study in a writing workshop, we begin by helping children develop a repertoire of strategies for collecting entries— this time, entries that can grow into essays. It's important to teach students that their lives are provocative. Writers observe things in the world, recording what we see, and then we shift and write, "The thought I have about this is…" or "This makes me realize…." When teaching children to grow essays out of everyday observations, we are really teaching them to free write, the goal being to help them realize the value of keeping at it, writing without a preconceived content but trusting that ideas will surface as they go along. Children can observe and then write their ideas about anything that is before them in the writing workshop, but they can also learn the power of imagining themselves in a provocative place and generating ideas in response to what they "see."

During this early phase of the unit, we also teach children that they can reread entries they collected earlier in the year during narrative units of study and use those entries as starting points, perhaps again beginning, "The idea I have about this is…" or "The thing that surprises me about this is…." A child might jot down a topic, hobby, or issue that he or she cares about, then collect ideas about that big subject and write about one of them. Children should become accustomed to selecting the strategy that works best for them on any given occasion. That is, the strategy the teacher introduces in a minilesson on a particular day is not that day's assignment but joins a growing repertoire of strategies that writers draw on as needed.

Essayists need tools to push past their first thoughts, and many find it helps to use thought-prompts to prime the pump of their thoughts. "The surprising thing about this is . . ." an essayist might write in his or her notebook before spinning out a brand-new thought in letters that scrawl down the page. The important thing will be that once a child records an idea, the child has strategies to elaborate upon that idea. Using prompts such as "to add on . . . ," "furthermore . . . ," "this makes me realize . . . ," "the surprising thing about this is . . . ," "on the other hand . . . ," "I think this is important because . . ." allows children to extend their first ideas and to use writing as a way of thinking. They find that new ideas come out of their pencils, ideas they never even knew they had.

After collecting possible seed ideas, young essayists select one and revise it until they've made a provocative, clear, compelling claim—or thesis statement. When it comes time for children to choose a seed idea, it helps to remind them that they already know how to reread their notebooks looking for seeds. In the earlier, narrative units of study, they selected a seed *story*; this time they will select a seed *idea* (a thesis).

Once students have selected and articulated an idea (it is hard to be an only child, for example), we teach them to elaborate on it by generating subordinate ideas (it's hard to be an only child because you get more attention than you want, it's hard to be an only child because you're often lonely, and so forth). The easiest way to support most claims is to provide a few parallel *reasons* for that claim; writers can restate the claim each time and add the transitional word *because* followed by a reason.

Usually children write support ideas through a series of parallel statements. One writer's thesis was, "It's hard being an only child," which she then elaborated on by saying, "Your parents shower you with

too much attention, your parents have too many of their hopes attached to you, and you can be very lonely."

During this planning stage, students can play around with their subordinate ideas and decide what they really want to say. In the end, we hope each child has a main idea (a claim or a thesis) and several parallel supporting ideas. We sometimes refer to the main idea and supporting statements as "boxes and bullets." We have found it helps if children take their thesis and record it on the outside of one folder, then make internal folders for each of their bullets (these become topic sentences for their body paragraphs).

When it is time for children to collect materials to support their topic sentences, we teach them that they can first collect stories that illustrate their ideas. It is also important to teach children to angle these stories so they support the idea the writer wants to advance.

Writers can also collect lists to support their topic sentences. We show children how statistics, observations, citations, quotations, and so forth can enrich their work. These bits are collected not in a writer's notebook but on separate bits of paper and filed in the appropriate topic-sentence folder.

It is important to help writers select *compelling* evidence from the material they collect in these folders, and to help them ensure that the evidence closely supports their claim. We teach them to look carefully from the claim to the evidence and back again, because often the two aren't as congruent as they appear at first glance. Eventually we teach writers to sort through the materials in each folder, writing well-structured paragraphs. Special lessons on transitions, introductions, and conclusions are important here.

Once writers have selected the most powerful and pertinent support material for each of their topic sentences, they staple or tape or recopy this information into a paragraph or two that supports each topic sentence, and in this manner construct the rough draft of an essay.

This unit ends with children learning that the long, involved process they've used to write personal essays can be abbreviated in order to write "instant essays." Writers learn not only *how* but also *when* to do this. This work is described in Chapter 11 of this book.

January

UNIT 4: WRITING FICTION: BIG DREAMS, TALL AMBITIONS

After students spend a month writing essays, they'll be eager to return to the land of narrative writing, especially if they are finally, at long last, able to write what students want to write most: short fiction. By this time, students will not be surprised that the unit begins with them learning ways to live like fiction writers, seeing ideas for stories everywhere. At the start of this unit, we let students know that fiction writers get ideas for their stories by paying attention to the moments and issues of our lives. We tell children, "When I was young, I thought fiction writers looked up into the clouds and imagined make-believe stories about castles and puppy dogs. But then I grew up and learned how real fiction writers get their ideas." We let them know that Robert McCloskey got the idea for *Make Way for Ducklings* when he was stopped in Boston traffic while a line of ducks waddled across the street in front of him.

Children collect story ideas in their writer's notebooks, learning to flesh the ideas out a bit so that they contain some of the elements of an effective story. Children learn to take the tiny details and big issues of their lives and speculate on how that could become stories. They might write entries in which they both recount a bit of their lives and then speculate (in writing) on how they could turn this into a story. A child who has recently moved could make up a story about a girl who moved, only this time she could give that girl a companion—a dog? a sister?—the writer wished she'd had. Children can reread their notebooks as well as live their lives collecting possible story ideas. In these entries, children will probably not actually write their stories; instead they will write plans for how their stories might go.

For a few days, children will collect entries in which they explore ideas that could possibly become fiction stories. As they do so, they will profit from trying story ideas out. A great way for them to do this is by "storytelling" those ideas to a partner. We teach children some storytelling techniques—for example, the beginning of their stories might sound like the beginning of a famous book or a fairy tale ("Once, not long ago, a little girl named Cissy…"). Elevating storytelling a bit helps each youngster bring a storyteller's voice—and an aura of literary language—to his or her own story plans.

Once children have each chosen a seed idea (which will now be called their story idea), it is important for children to develop those ideas. One way fiction writers do this is to develop their main characters, perhaps in notebook entries that never appear in the final story. A fiction writer once said, "Before you can begin writing your story, you need to know your characters so well that you know exactly how much change each one has in his or her pocket." When children are asked to develop ideas about their characters' traits, most children immediately list external traits (she has red hair, and so on). We encourage children to think also of a character's internal traits. What is she afraid of? What does she want? The trick is to help children create coherent characters with characteristics that fit together in a way that seems believable. When children use broad generalizations (for example, suggesting the character is a good friend), we ask them to open these terms up, to be much more specific (what are the unique ways in which this character is a good friend?). After writers gather entries developing their character, we may dramatize the character, having him or her perform action in a scene (a fiction writer's word for a small moment story).

Finally, it is important to be sure that young fiction writers think especially about a character's wants and needs. Usually a story line emerges out of the intersection of a character's motivations and the obstacles that get in her or his way.

Children use "story mountains" to plot the points of their stories and revise their story plans; these story mountains become the road maps for the stories. We help children see that these story mountains build to a high point and that their main characters make harder and harder climbs toward their goals. As they sequence their story, children learn that at the top of their mountain something happens that solves (or begins to solve) the character's problem and that when the character reaches the bottom, both the character and the reader should be satisfied with the journey.

Finally, children begin to draft their story, writing across the pages of a story booklet. Since the stories will be long, revision needs to begin early; it shouldn't wait until they've already written ten pages of text. We help students incorporate qualities of good writing as they revise the early sections of their stories. Children incorporate all they learned during the personal narrative units of study in their efforts to write short fiction. They use dialogue and small actions to draw their readers immediately into the story. They show rather than summarize character's feelings.

There are new lessons that children need to learn as they draft and revise fiction. For example, many children need to realize that a story can begin midpoint in a sequence of events, and that the opening scene can convey backstory. They need to learn to convey the passage of time, and to abut one focused scene against another. Above all, children are led to rethink the evolution of a story. Oftentimes, they approach a fiction story planning for the character to magically receive his or her fondest dream, often in the form of a solution that flies in out of nowhere like Superman. With help, we show children that in fiction as in life, the solutions we find are generally those that we make, and if there are magic answers to be found, they usually have been there before our eyes all along.

February

UNIT 5: LITERARY ESSAYS: WRITING ABOUT READING

In their personal essays, many children will have written about lessons they learned from people they know and interact with. But writing also helps us learn from the characters in the books we read. Just as writing allows us to pause in our hurried lives and really notice and experience and reflect on things that have happened to us, so, too, writing is a tool we can use to pause in our hurried reading and really pay attention to the characters in our books.

In order for children to write about reading in this way, they need to be reading! Children who are learning to write literary essays while they are still very young—in grades three, four and five—will profit from writing these essays about short texts they've read, reread, and discussed. In this unit, we invite children to read and study from small packets of short texts that merit close study. A teacher might thread one short story through many minilessons, showing children how she or he reads, thinks, and writes about that one story and then suggesting that children try similar techniques with a story from their packet. The stories in a child's packet need to be ones he or she can read. Therefore, children may not all have the same collection. We encourage teachers to provide stories that are rich, complex, and well crafted enough to reward close study.

On each of the first few days of the unit, we demonstrate a lens that readers can bring to a text, reminding children that all of these lenses accumulate so they have a repertoire of possibilities to choose from whenever they read. We teach children that just as essayists pay attention to our lives, expecting to grow ideas from this wide-awake attentiveness, so, too, literary essayists pay attention—but this time, the attention is directed to texts. Each child chooses a story that especially speaks to her or him and then collects entries about that story. The process of choosing a seed idea in this unit has two stages. First, a child chooses a story. Then, the child lives with that one story and gathers entries about it. Eventually, the child rereads those entries to choose a seed idea.

We remind children of their work in the personal essay unit, when they observed their lives and then pushed their thinking in their notebooks by writing, "The thought I have about this is . . ." or "This makes me realize that . . . ." In this unit, children can pause as they read to observe what is happening in the text and then develop an idea using the same conversational prompts. We teach children that their thoughts can be extended by using phrases such as "another example of this is," "furthermore," "this connects with," "on the other hand," "but you might ask," "this is true because," and "I am realizing." If we hope children will write literary essays in which they articulate the lessons they believe a character learns in a story or name the theme or idea a text teaches, then it is important to provide children with strategies for generating these sorts of ideas.

After children have collected reading responses in their writer's notebooks for at least a week, we remind them that they already know how to reread a notebook in order to find a seed idea. In the personal essay unit, students found seed ideas, and they'll need to do something similar now. We encourage students to search for a portion of an entry that tells the heart of the story in one or two sentences. We ask them to look for a seed idea that is central to the story and provocative.

We also help children generate possible seed ideas. I sometimes recommend that children try writing inside this general structure: This is a story about [identify the character] who [has this trait]/[wants/cares about such-and-so] but then [what happens to change things?] and s/he ends up [how?]. In other words, we may encourage students to try writing a sentence or two in which they lay out what the character was like at the start of the story, what happened to change things, and how this was resolved at the end: "*Because of Winn-Dixie* is the story of a lonely girl, Opal, who befriends a stray dog, Winn-Dixie. The dog helps Opal make friends with lots of people." "'Spaghetti' is the story of a lonely boy, Gabriel, who learns from a tiny stray kitten to open himself to love." I also encourage children to think of a story as containing an external as well as an internal story line, and to write an essay which highlights the internal (and therefore, sometimes the overlooked) story.

We help each child revise his or her seed idea so that it is a clear thesis, making sure it is a claim or an idea, not a fact or a question. We help children imagine how they can support the thesis in a few para-

graphs. Usually for children in grades three through five, the first support paragraph will show how the child's claim was true at the start of the story, and the next support paragraph(s) will show that it was true later in the story as well. It may be that the first support paragraph shows how the claim was true for one reason, the next, for a second reason.

Once children have planned their "boxes and bullets" for a literary essay, they will need to collect the information and insights they need to build a case. We encourage each child to make a file for each topic sentence and each support paragraph. For example, if the child's claim is "Cynthia Rylant's story 'Spaghetti' is the story of a lonely boy who learns from a tiny stray kitten to open himself to love," the child might title one file "Gabriel is a lonely boy" and another "Gabriel learns from a tiny stray kitten to open himself to love."

We also teach writers how to cite references from a text and how to "unpack" how these references address the relevant big idea. Before this unit is over, we teach children that writers of literary essays use the vocabulary of their trade, incorporating literary terms such as *narrator, point of view, scenes,* and the like. We may also want to teach students to write introductory paragraphs that include a tiny summary of the story and closing paragraphs that link back to the thesis and that link the story's message to the writer's own life, or to another story, or to literature as a whole.

March/April

A HOMEGROWN UNIT: POETRY

It would be incomprehensible to lead a yearlong writing workshop and not invite children to spend a month delving into a study of poetry. We didn't write this unit for several reasons.

First, it seems right that we provide fairly detailed support for half a dozen units of study and also leave space for you to author some of your own units of study. And what unit could be more satisfying to plan than a unit in poetry?

Then, too, we are confident that there are especially wonderful resources already available to help teach this unit of study. The unit on poetry that Stephanie Parsons and I wrote for *Units of Study for Primary Writing* could easily have been written for upper-elementary students; many teachers have that series in their schools. Our close friend and former Project staff member Georgia Heard has written two books (*For the Good of the Earth and Sun, Awakening the Heart*) that provide detailed help either in enriching that unit or in writing a new one. These books are available from Heinemann. In addition, draw on your own experiences writing poetry. You may find it helpful to read the summary below of one way in which this unit of study could unroll.

In a poetry study, children again practice all that they've learned thus far. Just as they have in all the previous units, youngsters will live like writers, finding significance in the ordinary details of their lives, gathering entries and images and lists that might be turned into publishable texts.

We may teach children to look carefully at everyday objects and pay close attention to their surprising beauty, to reconsider memories, to ponder conversations. They can also search for poems in past entries. A teacher may make this unit a time for close observation, teaching students to look for objects or scenes that capture their attention and intrigue them. (For examples of close observation poetry, see Valerie Worth's *All the Small Poems and Fourteen More*.)

All through the unit, children will read poems out loud so that they can learn how to savor the sounds of words. We can help them talk and think about the difference in sound and meaning between *fry* and *sizzle*, *shine* and *sparkle*, *cry* and *weep*. Ideally, they'll hear how the right choice of words can make a poem funny or wistful or sad. They'll learn how to create "mind pictures" by bumping an ordinary thing up next to something it's never been compared to before: "Today the sky looks soft and worn, like my old baby blanket." Children learn how to shape words on the page so that their texts not only sound but also *look* like poems. They learn that poets think about where to break a line so that

the sound, rhythm, and look of each line achieve the overall tone and meaning that the poet wishes to convey. They learn how poets use the white space around the words to pause, take a breath, and make something stand out from all the other words. For many children, all of the year's lessons in word choice, writing with detail, and making mind pictures suddenly make sense in the context of a small, shapely poem.

The teachers I know emphasize free verse. Rhyming well is a precise skill that many adult poets find difficult to master! We teach children to aim first for meaning—to find a way to describe what matters with words that will make the reader see the world in a brand-new way.

Once students have many beginnings and first tries of poems in their notebooks, we teach them that as poets draft new poems and rework poems they have already written, they try out many different versions. Poets make changes to better express what they most want to convey to the reader. They sometimes find that the act of revision brings new and more powerful ideas: what they want to say may change as they play with the way they're saying it.

Above all, the secret of poetry is heart. Poets write from the heart. Poets teach all of us to look at the world differently. They help us celebrate small beauties. They inspire us to be outraged over injustices great and small. And so, in this unit, we focus on the work that poets do in the world, the way that poets love the world through words, the way poets sustain us in hard times, the way poets express outrage and grief and joy.

April/May

ANOTHER HOMEGROWN UNIT: TEACHERS' CHOICE

A yearlong curriculum in teaching writing wouldn't be complete unless a group of colleagues have the chance to author your own unit of study in which you take your passions and your students' passions and fashion them into your very own unit of study. For this reason, I've deliberately left this month absolutely open. Chapter 9 in this book helps you imagine possible units of study you could coauthor with your colleagues.

There are endless possibilities for this unit. In some schools, teachers devote this time to a unit on content-area writing, taking down the walls between social studies (or science) and writing and inviting children to write about a subject the class has studied. These teachers sometimes ask children to write essays linked to the content area. Sometimes, instead, they invite children to explore the wide variety of forms in which nonfiction texts can be written. Journalism is an especially popular unit of study. Some teachers embrace the idea of Writing to Make a Real World Difference: Editorials, Persuasive Letters, and Feature Articles as a way to teach children to create on-the spot expository pieces.

In other schools, teachers who are eager to venture away from specific genres decide to focus this unit on a part of the writing process rather than on a genre. For example, some teachers use this time to teach students to live writerly lives; they ask children to renew their attachment to the writer's notebook and their commitment to wide-awake living, this time emphasizing that in real life, writers often begin with something to say and select a form that reflects their content and their purpose. Some teachers decide to embrace a unit of study on revision, perhaps designing a unit not unlike the revision unit in *Units of Study for Primary Writing*.

Other teachers use this time to focus on an aspect of writing: writing with literary devises, writing with a variety of punctuation, (see Angelillo) showing rather than telling. Still others focus on an author study, inviting all children to participate in a shared apprenticeship to one author. That shared apprenticeship might also be the focus of whole-class minilessons while each child (or small group) chooses a separate author. Some teachers use M. Colleen Cruz' *Independent Writing* as a reference and teach a unit of study on writing with independence.

Whatever unit a group of colleagues decides to pursue, the process of designing that unit will probably follow a course similar to the one I outline in Chapter 9.

May/June

UNIT 6: MEMOIR: THE ART OF WRITING WELL

This final unit aims to teach children that they can compose not only pieces of writing but also a life in which writing matters. Children will write a memoir, and in order to do so, they will draw on everything they have learned all year, and they will also invent more strategies and imagine more possibilities. At the start of the unit, we invite children to search for Life Topics. We suggest that Life Topics can be found by rereading our notebooks, reconsidering our lives, and living, wide awake to the topics that feel intensely alive and close to the heart. But we also tell children, "This time, you need to compose a writing life for yourself. You can draw on any strategy you have learned this year, or invent another strategy. Your job is to compose a writing life for yourself, one which is exactly tailored to you as a writer."

This unit, then, recognizes that the scaffolds that we have provided for children all year long can also become boxes, and the unit encourages children to set aside scaffolds that limit, and to realize that writers not only create texts, we also create our own writing lives.

We help children learn that in order to put themselves on the page with honesty and intensity, they need to write within a community of trust. And so now, as children 'round the final bend of the year, we again teach them what it means to really listen to each other and to themselves.

When writers really listen to themselves and each other, an entry or a topic can grow in significance. We encourage writers to use writing as a way to develop their own ideas and associations around a Life Topic, writing-to-learn in their writers' notebooks. In some classes, children in this unit of study refer to their seed idea as a 'blob' idea, imagining a glowing, living, changing heartlike form. Children learn that the process of 'choosing' a seed idea is a more flexible one than they'd at first learned, for as they live with a Life Topic, their sense of what it is they really want to say changes.

In this unit, children search for and create the forms for their writing. That is, we do not say to them, "This is how your writing will be structured." Instead, we teach children that writers often begin with a topic, and then choose or create forms that allow us to say whatever we want to say. Some children will write their narratives as a story, some will write a collection of short texts, some will write essays that are more journeys-of-thought rather than traditional thesis-driven essays. Mostly, children learn that the structures they've learned to use throughout the year are not as inflexible as they once thought, and they create texts which are hybrids, containing perhaps one long narrative section set off against a thesis-driven expository paragraph rather than a thesis-driven essay. As children create structures that will support their content, they learn about revision in a whole new way. They come to understand that writing is a process of growing meaning, and that writers use strategies as needed, as we reach to create meanings which feel deeply significant and personal.

CHAPTER 5

PROVISIONING A WRITING WORKSHOP

In 1986, when I wrote the first edition of *The Art of Teaching Writing*, I emphasized the importance of simple and predictable workshops. Over all these years I have continued to believe that teachers and children both profit when our writing classrooms are structured in clear, predictable ways. Back then, I wrote:

> If the writing workshop is always changing, always haphazard, children remain pawns, waiting for their teacher's agenda. For this reason and others, I think it is important for each day's workshop to have a clear, simple structure. Children should know what to expect. This allows them to carry on; it frees the teacher from choreographing activities and allows time for listening. How we structure the workshop is less important than that we structure it. (25–26)

I also said:

> [T]he most creative environments in our society are not the kaleidoscopic environments in which everything is always changing and complex. They are, instead, the predictable and consistent ones: the scholar's library, the researcher's laboratory, the artist's studio. Each of these environments is deliberately kept predictable and simple because the work at hand and the changing interactions around that work are so unpredictable and complex. (12)

In this chapter, I describe, in-depth, a workshop environment.

THE CLASSROOM ENVIRONMENT

Teaching writing does not require elaborate methods or materials or special classroom arrangements. Teachers who teach in widely divergent spaces and ways can all lead writing workshops, and their workshops can be more or less formal and traditional. There are, however, a few ways of organizing materials and space that are so supportive that these room arrangements and routines have become widely associated with writing workshops.

One necessary structure underpinning the units is the creation of long-term writing partners. These liaisons last at least across a unit of study and sometimes across several; they are not ability-based, nor does one child function as the "teacher," the other, the "student." In many classrooms, one partner is Partner 1, the other, Partner 2. On any one day, only one of the partners is apt to share, while the other listens and supports. To be sure that the more garrulous child doesn't always step into the spotlight, teachers specify who will talk and who will listen. "Partner 2, read your lead to Partner One, 1 will you talk about...." Usually teachers form these partnerships with an eye toward combining youngsters who'll do good work for and with each other. Partners do not write collaboratively, but they function as audiences for each other's writing-in-progress and frequently make suggestions to each other. In some classrooms, when work is published and celebrated at the end of the unit, the partner as well as the writer sits in the place of honor, and both writers are applauded for a job well done.

Room Arrangements

Many teachers arrange their classrooms to support a rhythm of children gathering for brief bouts of direct, explicit instruction, then dispersing for longer stretches of independent, partnered, and small-group work.

THE MEETING AREA Many teachers create a carpeted corner that serves at different times as a library, a meeting area, an arena for direct instruction, a place for reading aloud and giving and listening to book talks, and a quiet workspace. During minilessons, the teacher usually sits in a chair (kept nearby) and has both a chalk tray and a storage area of materials close at hand. Usually there is also an easel holding a giant pad of chart paper within reach. Some teachers also have an overhead projector at the ready, perhaps perched on top of a readily accessible bookcase, angled to project transparencies of student work or the teacher's writing onto the white board. An overhead projector, however, is totally expendable, and I urge teachers not to over-rely on it; too many projected images can make a minilesson feel more like a board meeting than a huddle among teammates.

When children gather for minilessons or share sessions, they usually sit in a clump or in rows on the carpet, drawn as closely as possible around the teacher. Most teachers assign children spots on the rug, moving the children who might otherwise sit on the fringes front and center. Each child sits beside his or her long-term partner.

Sometimes teachers tell us they do not have enough space for a carpeted meeting area. It is true that as our children grow older and our class rosters become longer, it can be more and more challenging to create a meeting space large enough to convene the class. On the other hand, as students get older, gathering and holding their attention becomes even more of a challenge, and a sense of community becomes all the more necessary. Because it is far easier to communicate with a whole class of students when they are pulled very close around us, teachers sometimes invent ways to make this possible. Many question whether they need a large teacher's desk at the front of the room and whether they need desks to be arranged so that all children can see the board (perhaps instead a system can be devised so that a few children know to move in a specified way when the teacher does frontal teaching with children at their workspaces). Tables and desks can be more easily consolidated into three quarters of the room if some space-hungry chairs are eliminated. By making some tables coffee-table height and positioning them along the edges of the meeting area, children at these tables can sit on the floor (perhaps on pillows) rather than on chairs—and the tables make perfect benches during meeting times. In other classrooms, children know the signal to convene means that half the class will squeeze onto a small patch of floor, another group will sit on turned-around chairs, and a third group will perch on the edges of a few well-placed tables. Whatever system the class agrees on, the important things are that the teacher can gather the children close and command their attention and the children can get themselves in and out of the configuration efficiently.

WORK AREAS   Although the meeting space is important, the most important thing is the rhythm of children sometimes pulling close around the teacher for a short stretch of very clear, explicit instruction, then dispersing to their workplaces, the teacher now meeting with individuals and sometimes with small groups of children as they write. That is, the rhythm in a writing classroom should *not* be three minutes in which the teacher talks, elicits, and assigns, then three minutes in which the children work, then three more minutes in which the teacher again talks, elicits, or assigns, followed by another three minutes of "seat work," and so on. Instead, teachers teach explicitly for about ten minutes, then children disperse to work on their writing for forty minutes before the teacher either convenes the class for a concluding meeting or asks writers to work with their partner.

In many classrooms, children write at tables or at desks that have been clustered together to allow table-like seating. (It is important for teachers to check out the relative position of chairs and desks, making sure that no child is writing at armpit level! Try doing this yourself for five minutes, and you will quickly see this is not too fine a point.) During the writing workshop, children often sit beside their long-term writing partner. Many teachers ask children to use children "assigned writing spots" that are different from their permanent seat. If children "own" the inside wells of their desks, but the desktops are in the public domain, children can sit in different arrangements at different times of the day. Alternatively, children's permanent seat arrangements may

reflect their partnerships, with each child sitting throughout the day alongside his or her writing partner.

As I will describe in more detail later, a writing workshop is usually punctuated by a brief mid-workshop teaching point. At this time, teachers often ask children to join their writing partners to do a particular bit of work. For example, after twenty minutes of writing, a teacher might ask for every child's attention, make a brief speech about the importance of writing with punctuation, and then ask children to double-check that both members of each partnership are using end punctuation. It is important that partners are able to convene and disperse efficiently. If partners *aren't* sitting alongside each other, they usually have prearranged "meeting spaces"—a neutral patch of floor or one partner's permanent seat.

CONFERRING AND PEER CONFERRING AREAS   While children are working, the teacher moves among the workspaces in order to confer with individuals and partnerships, carrying along a small chair or a stool in order to do this comfortably. In most classrooms, teachers work with small groups by gathering a cluster of children into little circles in the meeting area or in any spare section of floor space; some teachers do small-group work at a table designated for that purpose.

I discuss what happens during teacher-student conferences and small groups in another section of this book. Conferences, small-group strategy lessons and minilessons are absolutely crucial to a writing workshop.

THE WRITING CENTER   Different teachers have different ideas of what a writing center is. For some, a writing center is a place for a small group of children to sit when they write, while other groups of children do other activities at other centers in the room. This idea of a writing center fits with the concept of language arts instruction in which the teacher works with one reading group after another while the rest of the children work independently on various other literacy activities. These teachers have decided to let writing take place without explicit instruction and without the benefits of the larger community.

For writing workshop teachers and other teachers who prioritize writing instruction, a writing center is something quite different: it is a writing supply area. The writing center is where supplies that are not site-specific are kept. For example, the three-hole punch might be here, along with the boxes containing cumulative folders, copies of touchstone texts, and paper of different shapes and sizes (this is more common in the primary grades). Books on writing well, grammar guides, dictionaries, and thesauruses might also be shelved in a writing center. But I'm spilling over into the topic of writing materials, which is dealt with immediately below.

MATERIALS

When writing is an important part of the literacy curriculum, it is crucial for the teacher to develop a system for managing children's actual papers. I suggest that each upper-elementary student needs to have a writer's notebook, a writing folder for writing-in-progress, and a cumulative writing folder or a portfolio for stored, completed writing.

Writer's Notebooks

Some schools order a writer's notebook for each child, but in most schools teachers show children a variety of optional notebooks and then ask them to purchase their own. The dimensions and binding matter: the notebooks should have room for a lot of writing. (The dainty four-inch-square diaries with a lock and key don't give children the space they need, and their bindings often keep the pages from lying open on the desk or table while the child writes.) Many teachers also steer children away from spiral notebooks, because they have a "required class work" feel—we're after a more magical aura. Ideally a writer's notebook gives the impression that it could have been the notebook of choice for one of the authors that a child loves most. This isn't always possible, however, so it is also fine to settle on the marbled-covered composition books that are readily available at stores everywhere—especially if children

personalize them, perhaps laminating a collage of pictures and words of wisdom onto the covers. Certainly children need to write, "If lost, return to So-and-So" inside the cover of the notebook. These are ways to help children bond with their notebooks, and this emotional attachment matters more than one could imagine.

Writing notebooks offer a subtle way to make assignments multi-level. Some teachers steer their struggling or younger writers toward slightly smaller and thinner notebooks. Some suggest that struggling writers skip lines while the rest of the children write on every line. If you ask every member of your class to write a page and a half entry for homework most evenings, you might nevertheless suggest to a particular child that it's easier to reread that child's writing if she skips lines. This is a way to make your assignments more multi-level. Obviously, if more inexperienced or challenged writers work in notebooks with a smaller page size, this, too, allows for assignments to be multi-level.

Children date each entry they write in their notebooks and generally proceed in order though the notebook. That way, teachers can readily see the amount of writing a child has done in a day or a week. (Teachers must also take into account the drafts written outside the notebooks.) Children in grades three through five will usually write at least a page a day in school (often more) and will often write approximately as much at home. It is common for children to fill two writer's notebooks in a year.

Writing-in-Progress Folders and Paper

In addition to a writer's notebook, each child will need a folder for drafts, rubrics, guide sheets, and mentor texts related to the current unit of study. Most of the teachers I know suggest using a two-pocket folder for storing these materials. Usually, during the first week or two of the unit children will do most of their writing in their writer's notebooks, and during the second half of the unit they will do most of their writing on draft paper that they keep in their folders. When children are writing in their notebooks rather than their folders, only the notebooks travel between school and home, with the folders for any one table of writers stored in a box or a tray and brought to the table for the writing workshop.

Children need loose sheets of lined paper on which to write their drafts. Teachers decide whether each child supplies her or his own or whether the paper is provided in a writing center stocked with writing tools and materials. In grades three through five, most children like to write drafts on white lined composition paper, unless they have access to computers. Often during the first unit or two, two pages of lined paper are each folded top to bottom and then combined to create little booklets, each containing four half-pages. Some teachers ask children write rough drafts on yellow paper, final drafts on white paper. I recommend using white paper for all writing because yellow paper is harder to read, especially if children are writing in pencil.

Cumulative Folders

When a unit of study ends with a publication party at the end of a month, children empty their writing-in-process folders. They staple or clip a sequence of rough drafts, mentor texts, and unit-specific rubrics together and file them in cumulative folders. Some teachers send a folder of work home after each publication party. Others keep all students' work in a cumulative file. Either way, children begin a new unit of study with freshly cleaned-out files. And either way, work is not sent home in dribs and drabs. Final drafts are published and eventually filed.

Writing Utensils

A wonderful thing about teaching writing is that it is easy to provision a writing classroom! Children need something to write on—and something to write with. Other than paper, the most important tools are writing utensils; although any writing utensil is acceptable, I recommend pens. Pencils smudge and break, require sharpening, are harder to read, and invite children to erase. We want to study our children's rough drafts

and revisions, so it is preferable for them to cross out rather than erase deleted sections of texts. Then, too, most of *us* prefer to write in pen rather than in pencil, so presumably children feel the same.

Teachers need to decide whether each child will purchase and keep track of her or his own writing utensils or whether there will be communal ownership. If children chip in to purchase a whole-class stash of pens or pencils, and if this stash is used to replenish cans kept in tool boxes, one for each writing table, this avoids the "He took my pen!" scraps. If children write with pencils instead of pens, it helps to keep a can of sharpened pencils at each table and to teach writers that if their pencil needs sharpening, they can simply put it in their "to be sharpened" can and take another sharp one. Otherwise it is not unusual to find the struggling writers spending lots of time at the pencil sharpener.

Some teachers like to have date-stamps on hand to make it more likely that students date their work. They aren't necessary, of course, but dating one's work makes it much easier to hold students accountable for being productive. We encourage revision when we supply writers with scissors and tape. We encourage stamina when we supply them with the staplers that turn loose sheets into booklets.

The particular system I describe here isn't essential. What is essential is that each child in the school needs to date each day's work; children's work needs to accumulate until the authors' celebration; after an authors' celebration, some work needs to accumulate as evidence of children's growth over time; and no work can be sent home until the first final draft has been published and until teachers have an opportunity to talk to parents about significant progress evident in children's spelling and writing. This usually means teachers keep work in school at least until Open School night, teacher-parent conferences, or grade-by-grade parent meetings. By then, explanations about the writing process will be accompanied by convincing evidence of growth. After that, student work does not go home in dribs and drabs but instead, after a celebration, certain work may go home in a folder bearing the name of the unit.

Chart Paper, Marker Pens, Easel

Teachers will need to have a supply of chart paper and magic markers for writing visibly on this paper, and the charts teachers make throughout a unit will need to be visible to writers. An easel is incredibly helpful in a writing workshop. Many teachers turn a magnetic white board into a large writing process chart, with a space down one side for each child's name. Children move their name-magnets from one column to another to signal their progress from one stage to another. This chart functions as a record of the whole class' progress through the writing process.

Exemplar Texts

Writers need to read widely, deeply, ravenously, and closely. A classroom full of wonderful writers is one in which teachers read aloud several times a day and the children, too, are passionate readers. Although children benefit from rich classroom and school libraries full of a great variety of texts, in order to learn to write well, children especially need to read texts that resemble those they are trying to write. And they need not only graze these texts but also study some of them incredibly closely, revisiting them time and again to learn yet more and more and more. The same text can be used to teach leads, semicolons, character development, showing-not-telling, lists, pronoun agreement, and a dozen other things. I've often led workshops for teachers in which I show how one single text can be the source for dozens of minilessons.

In addition to a wide, rich library, each teacher needs a short stack of dearly loved and closely studied short texts that he or she returns to over and over throughout the year. It is great if children have their own copies of these texts, and many teachers type up and duplicate exemplar texts (also called *touchstone texts*) so that each child can carry a copy of the text in her writing folder for reference. (This sometimes requires permission from the book's publisher.) It is important that the touchstone texts that weave through a year are not the same texts, year after year.

Word Walls, Dictionaries, and Thesauruses

Every writing teacher will want to find ways to encourage children to spell conventionally. Most teachers find it helpful to teach children the high-frequency words that constitute the majority of what they write. After teaching children to spell a specific high-frequency word, teachers often post that word on a large alphabetical "word wall," encouraging children to use this as a resource so that they always spell that word correctly, even in rough drafts. Often teachers add five new words to the word wall each week, deleting a few that no longer require attention. They may also send copies of the word wall home with children once a week so that children can study these words at home and refer to them in the writing they do at home. Word wall words are a perfect source for phonics lessons, because they contain chunks that can be applied to countless other words.

In addition to a word wall, a writing workshop needs dictionaries and thesauruses. Writers care about words and are willing to work hard to find just the right one. These tools help convey the message that words matter.

Writers don't need much: paper, a pen, a place to store yesterday's writing, a few wonderful published texts, a responsive reader of writing-in-process, crystal clear help in writing well, an anticipated audience—and time. Ideally, a writing classroom has a carpet on which to meet and an easel and a pad of chart paper around which to gather, but not much is called for! Because writers don't need much, it is entirely possible for a school system to provision writing workshops with all that is needed, and doing so is enormously important. I've watched writing workshops take hold within a year or two in every classroom up and down the corridors of a school, and when I try to discern the conditions that made it likely that teachers and children would embrace the writing workshop, one remarkably important feature was the fact that the provisions were available. Throughout the history of the human race, tools have made us smarter. The wheel, the stylus, the computer—these tools of the hand become habits of the mind, re-creating what it means to live and learn together. Teachers and school leaders, too, are wise to pay attention to the important work of provisioning writing workshops.

CHAPTER 6

MANAGEMENT SYSTEMS

When teachers hesitate to teach writing using a writing workshop approach, it's usually for one of two reasons. The first is time, which is discussed in a different section of this book. The other is the fear that a writing workshop will pose insurmountable management challenges. Teachers who worry in advance about classroom management are wise to do so, because it is never a small achievement to establish the structures and expectations that ensure that children work with engagement and tenacity. How could it not be tricky to build an environment in which twenty or thirty youngsters each work and live within the confines of a small room for six hours a day, one hundred and eighty days a year? This challenge is inevitably more taxing when the goal is not only for children to live alongside one another but also for each child to maintain his or her own greatest possible intensity and receptivity for learning. In order for each child to learn well, he or she needs an individual mix of silence and collaboration, time and deadline, resources and support.

Why do so many people assume that it is only novice teachers who struggle with classroom management? Why is classroom management regarded as a low-level skill when corporate management is considered an executive skill? If the people working under our direction were grown-ups instead of children, the job of managing them would be regarded as highly demanding leadership. Executives take courses on designing accountability structures, structuring workspaces, and holding workers accountable. As classroom teachers, we need to give equal attention to these issues. Teachers should assume from the start that classroom management will inevitably be a challenge.

This does not mean, however, that classroom management is more difficult when leading a writing workshop than when teaching writing using other systems and methods. There are many ways in which the systems and structures of writing workshop make classroom management easier as well as more challenging. The important thing to recognize is that workshop teachers rely on different tools and techniques for managing children than do teachers who teach from the front of the room.

Long before the school year begins, then, we need to give careful thought to how we will institute the systems that will make it likely that our children will sustain rigorous work. When we plan our writing instruction, we must plan not only the words out of our mouths—the minilessons and the conferences that will convey content about good writing—but also the management structures and systems that make it possible for children to carry on as writers, working productively with independence and rigor. The good news is that none of us must invent management systems *ex nihilo*.

I recently visited the classroom of a first-year teacher. The writing workshop was about to begin. "Writers," Manuel said, "in a moment, I'd like you to bring your writer's notebook and your pen to the meeting area. Put everything else away and show me you are ready." As he counted ("Five, four, three, two, one.") children hurried to clear off their workspaces. "Table Two," Manuel signaled, "let's gather." Soon Manuel had signaled four other tables as well, and each time he gestured, his children stood, pushed in their chairs, walked swiftly and directly to the meeting area, and sat cross-legged, shoulder to shoulder with a long-term writing partner. Manuel had soon taken his place in the author's chair. "Writers," he said, touching his eyes to signal that he wanted children's eyes on him. Almost every child turned in his direction. Manuel then began a ten-minute minilesson in which he named a strategy that writers often use, demonstrated that strategy, gave the children a few minutes of guided practice with the strategy, and invited his writers to add that strategy to their repertoire. Soon the children had dispersed to their writing spots, each hard at work on his or her ongoing writing project. None of them waited for Manuel to offer a personalized jump-start.

As I watched all this, I marveled that Manuel, a novice teacher, was teaching in such efficient and effective ways. Had someone sprinkled Miracle-Gro on him? I remembered with a pang my first years as a

teacher. "How did he get to be so good?" I wondered, but then I knew. Manuel is the teacher he is because although *he* is new to the profession, *his methods* are not new. His methods have gone through hundreds of drafts and have benefited from the legacy of scores of experienced teachers. This is how it should be!

In order to teach writing, we need to establish structures that will last throughout every day of our teaching. As I said earlier, the essential premise, one that undergirds any system of managing a writing workshop, is this: the writing workshop needs to be simple and predictable enough that children can learn to carry on within it independently. That is, children need to be taught how to self-manage.

Because the work of writing is complex and varied, because children need to be able to follow their texts toward meaning and because teachers need, above all, to be able to coach writers who are engaged in the ongoing work of writing, the writing workshop in most classrooms proceeds in a similar way through a similar schedule, using similar management structures. Managing a writing workshop becomes immeasurably easier if children are taught in similar ways through succeeding years, thus allowing them to grow accustomed to the systems and structures of workshop teaching. For this reason, it is easier to manage a writing workshop if children are also learning math, science, reading, and social studies within workshops!

MANAGEMENT THROUGHOUT THE MINILESSON

Most teachers find that it is helpful to circulate around the room five minutes before the writing workshop begins saying, "Five more minutes until writing," or something similar. This gives children time to finish up whatever they are doing prior to writing time. The workshop itself begins with the teacher using an attention-getting signal to secure writers' attention, and then asking them to convene. It is remarkably important for teachers to develop such a signal and to teach children that it is a meaningful one. The signal can be obvious. Most teachers simply stand in the midst of the hubbub and say, in a voice one notch louder than usual, "Writers . . . ." Some instead ask, "Can I have your eyes on me?" or the abbreviated version, "Eyes?" The important thing is that we use the signal we settle upon consistently and teach children to honor it. This requires that after we say, "Writers," we wait as long as necessary until every child has put his pencil or pen down, stopped talking, and looked at us. At the start of the year, we may need to wait as long as three minutes before further addressing the group.

Of course, waiting alone isn't enough: we also need to talk explicitly about our expectations. Some teachers are uncomfortable insisting on utter silence and therefore they speak over still-murmuring children. I'm convinced we do our children no favors when we collude with their tendencies to ignore our words. If our goal is to teach children that words matter, then our language, for a start, must mean something: when we ask for attention, we should expect that children will comprehend and honor our request. The same children who are "Teflon" listeners, regularly letting our instructions roll off without getting through, tend also to be "Teflon" readers, regularly moving their eyes but not their minds over the words on a page, then looking up to say, "I read it, honest; I just don't remember what I read." If we expect that we'll regularly need to repeat ourselves several times before children take in what we've said, we are enabling our students to live as if they have comprehension problems. The first step in remedying this is to develop a way to signal for children's attention.

Once we have our students' attention, we will probably want to ask them to take out materials they'll need for writing, and we'll no doubt want to convey that we hope they'll bring some of these materials to the meeting area. Many teachers have a ritual for mobilizing children for writing. "Please set yourself up for writing. Five (I love that you are getting your notebooks out of your knapsacks), four (thanks for remembering your folders as well as your notebooks), three, two (in a minute I'll be

calling you to the meeting area), one." If teachers want children to bring particular materials, they make a point of holding up those materials, creating a Technicolor illustration. Some teachers regularly list whatever they want children to bring to the meeting on a white board. This way, they need only say, "Let's gather," but children know this means they must check the white board and bring the listed items with them. In other classrooms, teachers expect each child to bring his or her writer's notebook, writing folder, and a pen or pencil to the meeting area, which of course means that children always have the basic supplies on hand.

If children do bring supplies to a meeting, the next question is: what happens to the supplies during the meeting? Do we want children to put their work on the floor in front or behind them? Literally sit on top their work? Any of these systems increases the chances that children won't be distracted by fingering through their materials. On the other hand, some teachers want writers to open their writer's notebooks before a minilesson starts and be ready to take notes.

In many classrooms, children gather on the carpet half a dozen times a day; it is obviously worthwhile to be explicit about how we hope they will do this. Experienced workshop teachers are apt to demonstrate—act out—showing children that they are expected to push in their chairs, make a beeline for their spot on the meeting area rug, sit (rather than hover), handle materials however they are expected to be handled, and begin rereading the charts containing teaching points from previous days. At the start of the year, after the teacher calls one table of writers to the meeting area, the teacher is apt to name (for the other writers) what children do well: "I love the way they pushed in their chairs, don't you? Look how quickly and quietly they're coming to the meeting area!" Of course, before long this behavior becomes automatic, and teachers merely need to say, "Table One, please join me," and children push in their chairs, come quickly and quietly, sit in their assigned spots, open writer's notebooks to the next available page, and begin rereading charts from previous minilessons. This is very efficient! In many classrooms, children are taught that when the teacher takes her place in the chair and says, "Writers," children should be sitting on their bottoms with their hands contained in their own space, looking at the teacher.

Some may question this detailed attention to how children move from one place to another, and there certainly will be teachers who prefer a more organic, easygoing approach. But for lots of teachers, especially those in crowded urban classrooms, transitions can be a source of delay and tension, and neither is advisable. A fiction writer once said, "The hardest part of writing fiction is getting characters from here to there," and this can be true for teaching as well.

I find it striking that in classrooms in which the transitions are long and mired in tension, teachers often assume this is par for the course. They shrug and say, "What are you going to do?" as if they assume this is how writing workshops proceed in most classrooms. I've come to realize that many aspects of classroom management are shaped more by our teaching and specifically our expectations, than by our children's developmental levels. When teachers make a point of teaching classroom management, thirty children can come and go quite seamlessly between the meeting area and their workspaces.

During minilessons, children usually sit alongside their partners. At the start of the minilesson, teachers typically talk about and then demonstrate a strategy; children are expected to listen, rarely to talk. Some children don't know that the start of a minilesson is a time for them to listen rather than talk. In those cases, the teacher might say, "You'll notice that at the start of a minilesson, I do the talking. This is my time to tell you something very important."

After talking and demonstrating, the teacher says, "Let's try it," or something of that nature, to signify that this is the Active Engagement section of the minilesson. Teachers set children up to be active during this time; usually this means either to "write in the air" or "turn and talk" with a partner. For example, if the minilesson taught that writers sometimes reread drafts, looking at action words and asking, "Is this the exactly true word?" the teacher would probably reread a draft of a few sentences in front of the class, pausing at each action word, musing

aloud whether it was the exactly true word. Then she'd say to the class, "So let's try it." She might set the class up to continue rereading the text, saying, "If you find a place where I used a generic word instead of a precise one, would you write in the air, showing your partner how you'd repair my draft," thereby channeling children to say aloud the word they recommend substituting. Alternatively, the teacher could ask children to notice and then discuss in pairs the steps she went through in order to replace a generic term with a precise one: "What steps did you see me taking when I replaced *went* with *crept*? Turn and talk with your partner."

Children need to know how to make a fast transition from facing forward and listening, to facing their partner and talking. Children can't spend five minutes getting themselves off the starting block for a turn-and-talk (or a stop-and-jot), because the entire interval usually lasts no more than three minutes! We need to teach children explicitly how to make the transition from listening to the teacher to interacting with a partner. I've watched teachers practice this with kids by saying, "What did you eat for breakfast this morning? Turn and talk," and then, after a minute, saying, "Back to me," and finally giving children feedback on their ability to shift between whole-class listening and turning and talking or jotting.

MANAGEMENT AT THE START OF WORK TIME

Once the minilesson is over, in a classroom in which some of the materials are centralized, table monitors distribute materials. That is, if folders are kept in boxes rather than in children's knapsacks, a table monitor will put a box of folders on each table. If tools are kept in a table-caddy, this will also be put on each table.

Just as we explicitly teach children how to gather for a minilesson, we also teach them how to disperse after the minilesson and get started on their work. The important thing is that children need to learn how to go from the minilesson to their workspaces, and then to open up their folders or notebooks, decide what they are going to do, *and get started doing it.* If we don't teach them otherwise, some children will sit idly by until we make our way to that table and give that child a personalized jump-start. Teachers have learned, therefore, that it is worthwhile to come right out and teach children how to get themselves started writing. Sometimes a teacher will disperse one cluster of writers at a time. While one cluster goes off to work, the teacher may say to those still sitting on the carpet, "Let's watch and see if they *zoom* to their writing spots and get started right away!" Sometimes the teacher will speak in a stage whisper ("Oh, look, Toni has her notebook open and is rereading the entry she wrote yesterday. That's so smart! I wonder if the others will do that? Oh, look. Jose is rereading too!"). This reminds both the dispersing and the observing youngsters what the teacher hopes they will do.

Sometimes teachers find it helpful to ask children first to envision what they will do that day. "Picture yourself leaving the meeting area. Where will you go, exactly? What will you do first? Thumbs up if you can picture yourself leaving and getting started," the teacher might say, signaling to the children who seem ready that they can go back to their writing spots.

Sometimes we disperse children by saying, "If you are going to be doing (one kind of work), get going. If you are going to be doing (another kind of work), get going. If you are not certain what to do today and need some help, stay here and I'll work with you." Soon we are leading a small group of children who've identified themselves as needing more direction.

Transitions are smoother if children always know where they'll sit during writing time. In most classes, children have assigned writing spots. But children also need help knowing what to do, especially in instances when the minilesson doesn't channel children in one specific direction. If children are in the earliest stages of work, they always know they can write a new entry, but once children have begun work on a piece, they are apt to be in the midst of revising. I usually tell children that if one is not sure what to do as a writer, the wisest thing is to reread recent writing, thinking, 'What does this piece need me to do next?' I

also suggest that if children are stymied, they can look at charts for strategies that writers often use and decide which of those strategies might work at that point for their particular piece. In some classrooms, children are expected to give themselves an assignment (also referred to as a planning box) each day. "Decide what you are going to do, record your plans in a self-assignment box, and get started! Walter Dean Myers doesn't wait for a teacher to appear at his elbow and to say, 'You can start now,' and you don't need to do this either."

In a classroom in which children tend to wait for individual jump-starts, I suggest teachers say to children, "At the start of each day's writing workshop, I won't be available for conferences. Instead, this is a time for me to admire and record the ways you get yourselves started in your writing."

MANAGEMENT DURING WORK TIME

What do I mean when I say that children give themselves an assignment? Isn't the teacher assigning the work through the minilesson?

In upper-grade writing workshops, children usually write one completed (final) piece each month. There are exceptions. During the *Launching* unit of study, I suggest that children (especially third graders) draft two personal narratives, choosing just one to revise and edit for publication. In a poetry unit of study, children will obviously write more than a single poem, and in a journalism unit, children will write many news articles. And when teaching a unit of study on revision, the teacher might ask children to look back over all the writing they've done all year and select, say, four pieces to put through further revisions. But on the whole, in a unit of study, upper-elementary students progress through the writing process and end up with one final piece. In a sense, the teacher "assigns" the writing of this one text.

In many units of study, the teacher has selected a genre of writing (or a structure of writing) for the entire class. That is, everyone may be writing a literary essay or a memoir or an editorial. There will sometimes be units of study which are open-genre (with each child deciding what form his content suggests), but it is more common for the class to investigate and write within a genre the teacher has selected. In a sense, the teacher "assigns" children to write within that genre.

Children are always expected to progress through a writing process that they learn about in the writing workshop. In the upper-grade classrooms I know well, each child is expected to live a writerly life, paying attention to what goes on around them day by day and collecting a variety of entries. Each child is expected to reread these entries and select one "seed idea" to develop in ways that match the genre (such as making a timeline if the genre is personal narrative), write a draft, then revise and edit that draft. In a sense, the teacher "assigns" children to work their way through this writing process.

But on most days, children still need to choose what it is they will do that day. Every child may know he or she needs to write a timeline for his or her story, consider whether the entire sequence represented in the timeline belongs in the story, choose some "dots" in the timeline on which to elaborate, try writing different lead sentences, study exemplar texts, and the like, but some children will spend more time in one portion of this work, some in another. And every writer is encouraged to use his or her judgment, making decisions about what the piece of writing needs and letting the piece of writing and the writer's own hopes come together in an individualized work plan.

The rule of thumb during a writing workshop is that during writing time, everyone writes. So there is no such thing as being "done." If a writer completes one thing, then he or she begins the next thing. On a given day, a writer might progress through a sequence of writing work. For example, a writer might study a few exemplar leads, try a few leads, select one, and start a draft.

As writers progress along through their sequence of work, many of them come to places where they feel stymied. "I'm stuck," they say. When a child feels stuck, the first instinct is usually to find the teacher and ask, "What should I do next?" These interactions between a writer and a teacher are referred to as conferences, and they may occur at the initiative of the writer or the teacher.

But in conferences (as well as in minilessons and small-group work), teachers explicitly teach children to be self-reliant writers and decision makers. In minilessons, teachers teach children what they can do when they feel stuck—or when they are done or when they don't know how to start writing or when they want to revise or when they encounter any of many other problems. Almost always, teachers teach children an array of expendable strategies that writers sometimes draw upon and then we expect children to draw on these strategies as needed to achieve goals which are not expendable. In conferences, teachers personalize this instruction, scaffolding children to become more self-reliant, strategic, and skillful writers.

Teach and Organize So That Children Rely on Each Other

If youngsters seem overly reliant on us for direction, we often teach them to help each other. "Writers, can I stop all of you? Would you look at all the people following me! I feel like a pied piper. Writers, today I want to teach you that there is not just one writing teacher in this classroom. Each one of you can be a writing teacher. And you need to become writing teachers for each other because this is how we learn to become writing teachers for ourselves—in the end, every writer needs to be his or her own writing teacher. So right now, let me teach you what writing teachers do for each other. Then those of you in this line behind me can help each other."

Teachers need to decide exactly what it is they think children in a particular class *can* do for each other. At a minimum, writers can listen to each other talk about their subjects. The first step in helping writers listen to each other is to teach children to ask open-ended questions. "Your job is to ask me questions that get me to talk at length about my subject. Ask questions that get me teaching you about the aspects of my subject that are important to me. Let's try it. I'll be a writer. 'I'm stuck. I don't have much to say. I wrote about my bike ride but nothing much happened. . . .' Remember, your job is to ask me questions to get me talking." One child asks, "How long did you ride for?" This is a closed question and we want children to ask open-ended questions. We answer curtly: "Two hours." "Was it fun?" Again, the question doesn't call for an expansive answer, so we don't give one: "Yes." Eventually a child will ask a more open-ended question: "What were the fun things about the bike ride?" "Oh! I'm glad you asked. I expected the bike ride to bring me into nature, but this particular bike trail was loaded with people, and it was almost as sociable as a neighborhood picnic." Children probably will have missed what we just tried to demonstrate so we come right out and name what we've done. "Do you see, writers, that Jeremy asked the kind of question that got me really talking? He didn't ask a yes-or-no question like, 'Do you like your bike?' Instead he asked, 'What were the fun things you did?' That's so helpful, because now I have ideas for what to write. And he could help me get even more ideas if he asked follow-up questions. Try it, Jeremy. Ask me to be more specific."

Children not only need to be taught to help each other in peer conferences, they also need a structure that allows them to do this. In some classrooms, children shift between writing and conferring as needed, and this can be workable. Sometimes, however, if children have standing permission to shift between writing and conferring, very little writing is accomplished, in which case teachers wisely insist that writers work silently, conferring only in specified areas of the classroom. For example, some teachers set two pairs-of-chairs up along the margins of the room; as long as two chairs in the "conference alley" are open, a writer and his or her partner can decide to meet for a five-minute conference (some teachers keep a timer in the conference areas to enforce this time constraint; others add the timer only if the length of conferences becomes a problem).

In addition to student-initiated conversations, teachers often ask the whole class to meet with their partners to discuss something specific.

Often these partner conversations follow a mid-workshop teaching point or come at the end of a writing workshop. That is, most writing workshops are punctuated by the teacher's standing up in the middle of the workshop hubbub, signaling for attention, and then giving a pointer. For example: "Most of you are having your character talk, including dialogue in your story, and that's great. But today I want to remind you that dialogue needs to sound right to the ear. It needs to sound like something a real human being would say. Get with your partner and read your quoted sections aloud to each other. Ask, 'Does this *sound like* a real human being?' If it doesn't, see whether you can alter the quoted section so that it does." A mid-workshop interruption like this sets partnerships up to talk with each other briefly about a topic the teacher specifies. Similarly, at the end of the writing workshop, teachers often ask partners to share with each other, "Find a place where your character's talk really rings true, and read that aloud to your partner. Then look together at what you've done and try to dissect why it worked." Of course, sometimes these interactions are more open-ended, "Writers, would you tell your partner what this mentor author has done that you'd like to emulate? Show your partner where in your draft you might use this technique."

Use Table Conferences and Strategy Lessons to Keep the Class as a Whole Productive

During a writing workshop, teachers spend most of their time moving among youngsters conducting brief conferences. I write about these conferences in a separate chapter, but for many teachers, the issue is not what to say in conferences. Instead, the problem is how conferences are possible in the first place; "What are the other children doing while I confer?"

True, teachers cannot devote themselves to one-to-one conferences until the whole class has learned to carry on as writers. On days when we know that lots of children are going to need our help, instead of conferring with individuals, we will probably decide to opt for the more efficient alternative of meeting with groups.

If, for example, we have just taught children that essayists elaborate on our thesis statements by making two or three parallel claims, each becoming the topic sentence in a support paragraph, we can anticipate that a third (or even half) of the class will need hands-on help translating our instructions into actions. With such a large-scale need for help, we will probably decide to blanket the room with "table conferences." Instead of gathering selected children together, we can go from one table to another, ask for every child's attention, then confer with one child who needs help while the others watch. Of course, the others will not want to watch unless we shift back and forth between demonstration and debriefing and do this work in a manner which helps not only the focal child but all the others who need similar help: "Do you see how Anthony just did such-and-so? Try doing the same thing right now." Then, as the children begin emulating Anthony's first step, I can help Anthony proceed to another step, one which the observing children see with only peripheral vision. Soon I'll point out to the table full of listeners that they, too, can do the work Anthony has just done.

I often blanket the room with table conferences during the first few days of the writing workshop and again at the start of each unit of study. At these times, there will be a reasonable chance that writers are all at the same place in their work, which is less apt to be true in the midst of a unit of study.

Another way to reach lots of writers efficiently is to sort them into need-based groups and gather each group for a brief strategy lesson. Again, I describe the methods and content of these lessons elsewhere; for now, the important thing to say is that we can easily lead four small-group strategy lessons in a single day. These are not formal events. Usually we convene the first group based on the student work examined the night before. Toward the

end of the minilesson, I am apt to call out a list of names and say, "Will these writers stay on the carpet after the minilesson?" Then I talk to this group: "I looked over your writing last night and I want to make a suggestion to all of you." I might show this group how they can get past their impasse and ask them to try what I suggested or demonstrated while they continue sitting together. As these children get started, I might move around the room, ascertaining what other children need. If I noticed, for example, one child who was writing without any punctuation, I might think to myself, "I wonder if there are others like this child?" Finding others with similar problems, I might gather this group. "I've been looking over your writing and I have one thing I want to teach you and to ask you to do." While this second group gets started, I might return to the first group. I might check in with each member of the group quickly, then say, "Can I stop you?" and make a point or two that pertains to them all. Alternatively, I might decide to confer with one child while the others watch, extrapolating larger points from this one situation.

In both of these instances, I set out to do small-group work. Sometimes, instead, we intend to conduct one-to-one conferences but find part-way through the workshop that we need to reach more children more efficiently and therefore shift into leading a small-group strategy lesson or two. We are wise to shift to small-group instruction when we find we are having what is essentially the same conference over and over. For example, if I have just helped one child who was writing about a giant topic—"My summer"—narrow it to something more focused and the very next child I approach needs the same kind of help, I am apt to say, "Will you wait for just one second?" while I peer over kids' shoulders to see which other children need the same help. Signaling, "Come with me," I soon have six children pulled into a tight circle on the carpet. Often I will then use the conference with the first child as a case in point.

Then, too, if I am trying to confer and can't because I am swamped with children who *all* need attention, I may triage these needy children and work with them in small groups. To one group, I'll say, "I called you together because it seems all of you are having a hard time getting much down on your page. We've been writing for twenty minutes today, and every one of you has less than a quarter of a page. So let me tell you ways that I get myself to write more, and then let's try those ways—because during writing time, writers need to write. One thing I do a lot when I'm having a hard time writing is thus-and-so." To another group, I might say, "I called you together because although you are writing up a storm and that's great, you are forgetting that writers try to use what we know about conventions as we zoom down the page. I don't want you to go to the opposite extreme and fuss over the shape of every letter and spend twenty minutes looking every word up in a dictionary, but I do want you to become accustomed to pausing for just a second as you write to ask, 'Did I spell that word right?' If you need to, you should be checking with the word wall as you write." I can also convene children who spend too long in their peer conferences, who never seem to light upon topics they care about, who forget their writer's notebook, who summarize rather than storytell in their narratives, who let dialogue swamp their stories, or who need to add transitions into their essays.

Support Students' Writing Stamina

What if children can't sustain work the whole time? Generally writing workshops involve ten minutes for a minilesson, forty minutes for writing and conferring (with a five-minute mid-workshop teaching point) and five or ten minutes for a culminating share session. At the start of the year, children who are new to a writing workshop may not be able to sustain writing for forty minutes. If children are not accustomed to writing for this length of time, after fifteen minutes the class will become restless.

If children have trouble with stamina, part of the problem will probably be that they are doing everything you suggest they do in such an underdeveloped fashion that the work is done within ten minutes. In that case we may decide to give them a series of additional directions (via mid-workshop teaching points) that will sustain them for several more short intervals. Setting up these mid-workshop teaching points for children to talk with a partner will give them a break from the physical act of writing as well as a chance to rehearse whatever they will write next.

We may also decide that for a few weeks at the start of the year our writing workshops will be briefer than they'll be once children have developed more stamina. Just don't let abbreviated work periods become the norm. Children will never write well if they are accustomed to writing briefly. Elaboration is one of the very first and most foundational qualities of good writing.

If you see that even after your children have been in a writing workshop for several months, they are still not producing even a page a day during writing time (and more text at home), then you'll want to intervene to increase the volume of writing your students do. Start by talking up the fact that writers, like runners, set goals for ourselves, and ask children to push themselves to write more. Then during the workshop, go around cheerleading children to write more. Make stars or checks on their pages when they produce a certain amount of text. Watch for when a child is pausing too much and whisper, "Get going!" Mid-way through the workshop, intervene to ask children to show with a thumbs-up, thumbs-down whether they've produced whatever the aspired amount of text might be. Use share times as a time to count (and even to graph) how many lines of text each writer produced. Solicit children who have increased their volume to talk about what they did to reach this goal. Make charts of "Strategies for Writing More." Eventually, if some children aren't getting enough writing done during writing time, ask them to return to their writing at another time of the day—during recess, before or after school. Say, "You wouldn't want days to go by without getting a chance to write at least a page," or, "Writers do this. We set goals for ourselves. Sometimes it does take us a while to get the words on the page, but that's okay. We just rearrange our day so that somehow, we get the chance to write." You'll find that the amount of writing your children do can be transformed in short order if you go after this goal with tenacity—and the same is true for almost any goal you take on!

MANAGING ONE-TO-ONE CONFERENCES

Although there are times when so many children need us that it is much more efficient to work with small groups than with individuals, one-to-one conferences must remain the mainstay of an effective writing workshop. The writing process approach to teaching writing is also called the conference approach for a reason: teacher–student conferences play a critical role in the entire enterprise. In a later chapter I talk about the internal structure or pattern of conferences. Here I describe conference management practices that help lead children to independence.

When we say that our children are not able to sustain work long enough to do much conferring, we need to look at ways in which we can scaffold children's independent work. Writing conferences, themselves, must be angled to teach children how to carry on with independence another time. Some conferences will begin with a writer coming to us and saying, "I'm stuck." Our first job is to learn what the writer has already done, has been trying to do, and has considered doing next. Then we need to help the writer extend his or her work in ways that make the writer more self-reliant in the future. "So you aren't sure what to do next. What I tend to do is reread my writing, starring the sections that I think really work and check-marking the sections that don't work so well. Then I decide which to work on first. Often I start with the sections that work well, and I think, 'How can I make these longer?' I ask, 'How can I make more of this good part?' Why don't you try that now? After this, when you aren't sure what to do, this is always something you can try."

Sometimes when we cannot carve enough time out of the workshop for one-to-one conferences with individuals, the underlying issue that keeps children from working independently involves not having the necessary materials readily available. If getting paper is a big problem in our class, our

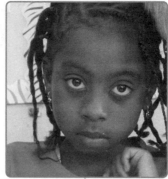

writers will be stymied and they'll all be at our elbow saying, "I need more paper." If we are the holder of the stapler, they'll line up behind us for staples.

Then, too, sometimes the issue is that children rely on us to help them come up with topics for writing. If we haven't taught children strategies for generating writing and for coming up with topics, then whenever a child is ready to embark on a new entry, that child will be at our elbow. If we haven't convinced children that we expect them to approximate spellings "as best they can" and keep going, then children will line up for help each time they come to a challenging word. Our goal is to enable writers to cycle through the entire process without needing help. Their independence gives us the time and freedom we need to be able to pull a chair alongside one writer and then the next, and to teach.

Choosing with Whom to Confer

Although the context for our conferences is created by the entire fabric of our teaching, conferring itself creates its own organizational challenges. For example, we will need to decide how we'll figure out which child to meet with next. Teachers develop their own idiosyncratic systems here. Some teachers enter a writing workshop with a little list in hand of writers they plan to see. The list may come from studying their records and noticing the children they haven't conferred with for a while and from thinking about previous conferences that need follow-up. Alternatively, the list may come from thinking about or reading through children's work and deciding on both children who need help and children who could, with help, do exemplary work that might fuel the next minilesson, mid-workshop teaching point, or share.

Personally, although I do enter a workshop with a list of the children with whom I hope to confer, I find it is important to be able to improvise based on the signals children give me. That is, if youngsters at one table seem unsettled, I'm apt to confer with a child at that table, knowing that my presence can channel the entire group to work rather than socialize. Then, too, if one child is especially persistent about needing help, I generally assume he needs to be a priority—unless he is always at my elbow, in which case I'll respond differently.

I tell children that if they need my help, they should get out of their seats and follow me as I confer. I find this keeps the child who feels stymied from derailing his or her companions as well; in addition, the children learn from eavesdropping on conferences. I also receive very tangible reminders of how many children feel confused or stuck at any moment, and this keeps me on my toes. If I have six children in tow, I'm not apt to overlook them for long.

Keeping Conference Records

We as teachers will definitely want to record our conferences, and it is important to develop a system for doing so that fits intimately into the rhythms of one's own teaching. The important thing is that the writing about teaching that we do must help us teach better and help our students learn better. This writing needs to be attuned to our teaching, reflecting, and planning. We will probably go through a sequence of systems before settling, temporarily, on one. Five or six systems are especially common among the teachers with whom I work.

Some teachers keep a page on a clipboard that looks like a month-at-a-glance calendar but is, instead, the class-at-a-glance. For the period of time this page represents (which tends to be two weeks) the teacher records the compliment and teaching point of any conference she holds. Sometimes the grid has light lines dividing each child's square into several parallel slots, with alternate slots labeled either *c* or *tp*.

Alternatively, teachers may carry a version of the record-keeping form included on the CD-ROM included with this series. Instead of recording what we say when we compliment and teach each new child, the teachers brainstorm what we are apt to compliment and teach (these

will be the same things, just at different times) within a unit. We turn this into a prewritten list of possible compliments or teaching points, and use this list to jog our mind as to possible things we can teach. Teachers carry these prewritten lists of teaching points with us, checking off what the child is doing that merits a compliment, what we teach, and what we recognize we *could* but won't be teaching.

Some teachers have notebooks divided into sections, one for each child, and record our conferences with each child that way. Others do a variation of this, recording the conferences on large sticky notes and later moving the note to the appropriate section of their notebook. Some teachers do an enlarged version: they post their conference notes on a wall-sized grid, which reminds every child what he or she has agreed to do—and serves as a very visible record of which children have and have not received this form of intense instruction. I like to record conferences in the student's writer's notebook, the logic being that this way when I return for another conference, I can look at both the conference notes and the ensuing work. At the same time, the child has a very tangible record of the agreed-on work and the pointers I have made.

MANAGING THE SHARE TIME

You will want to have two or three alternate ways that share time generally goes in your classroom and to induct children into those traditions right from the start. You will certainly want the option of convening children in the meeting area. The logistics of this will match those you rely upon to convene children for the minilesson. A child might circle the room when there is just three minutes left before the share session—either you'll ask this child to do this, or, if the times for writing in your classroom truly ascribe to the daily schedule, then it could be a child's regular job to keep track of time and initiate these rounds. Alternatively, you could intervene to announce, "Three more minutes." In any case, children will need a bit of time to finish what they are writing. Then you'll bring children to the work area. You may simply say, "Writers" to get kids attention and then use hand signals, or you may convene children by table. Either way, you'll want children to bring their work with them and to sit in their rug spots beside their partner.

If you've convened children in the meeting area, you'll probably plan to talk with them for a bit, and you may plan to share one child's work. You may read the child's work aloud yourself, or ask the child to stand or sit beside you (or in your place) at the front of the meeting area, and to share his or her work. Then, typically, you'll invite children to talk with their partner. You may recap by repeating something you overheard, but more likely, time will be running short so you'll simply sum up the day's work and make a transition to whatever you'll teach next.

Just as often, however, you will decide to lead your share session without convening children. You'll want to stand in some prominent spot, to use your attention-getting signal to gather children's attention, and then to wait until you really do have full attention. You'll know you have children's full attention because they won't be writing any longer and they will be looking at you. This will provide you with a context in which you can teach using normal intonation and volume, and it is important to do so. If you have made the decision to not convene your children, chances are good that you'll curtail the length of your remarks, and devote most of the share session to a partner share. Partners either need to be sitting alongside each other, or they need a plan for meeting together which does not entail moving furniture or taking more than a minute of transition time.

Finally, you'll probably want another format for share sessions, and you can select the format which works the best for you. Some teachers like to use partnership shares when children are sharing work, and use table-shares when children are talking over their ways of solving a particular writing problem. That is, if your goal in the share is to

encourage children to talk about how they are planning ways to end their stories, then you might suggest they have a table conversation about this. Some teachers use those table conversations as a prelude to a community meeting, which probably involves convening in the meeting area.

Alternatively, you may find that in your classroom, the ritual that I describe as a symphony works well. In this ritual, you ask children to search for an instance when they did something well. For example, you may have taught children that the way a character speaks, as well as the content of the character's language, needs to reveal the person. You may have asked children to find a place in their text where they use dialogue in ways that reveal the character. "When I tip my baton to you, would you read out one instance when you used dialogue to reveal character?" you could say, and then function like the conductor in a symphony, with one child after another reading a contribution.

Teachers that I know have devised a few other alternate rituals for share sessions, and you should certainly see this as one more place where you can draw on your own imagination of what's possible. Whatever you devise, however, I encourage you to be sure that you often use this same mechanism for sharing and getting responses to writing. If every day's writing workshop ended with a chance for writers to meet with a partner and to talk about whatever is on the writer's mind, those partnership meetings could still be endlessly interesting for children.

CHAPTER 7

THE PATTERNS OF MINILESSONS

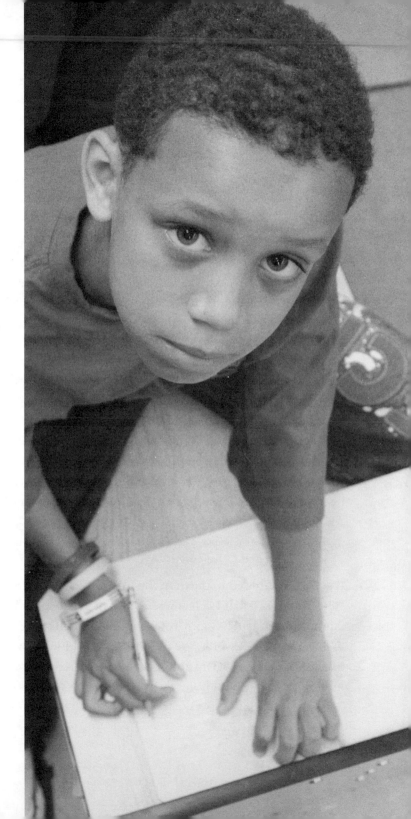

Just as the art instructor pulls students together to learn a new glaze technique or a new way to mix paints, just as the football coach and his team huddle over a new play, so too the teacher of writing pulls children together for a minilesson which opens each day's writing workshop.

Minilessons power our curriculum. Once we learn how to lead strong, efficient minilessons, we find we have a power chip that never quits. It generates strong teaching each day, each year. The teachers I teach worry most over how they'll generate the *content* for their minilessons. I'm convinced, however, that it's equally important for teachers to learn the *methods* of leading efficient, effective minilessons.

Our most effective minilessons tend to follow a similar template. That is, while the content of the minilessons changes from day to day, the architecture of minilessons remains largely the same. The minilesson that follows illustrates the major components of most minilessons.

THE ARCHITECTURE OF A MINILESSON

Once the youngsters have settled onto their rug spots, I took my place and said, "Writers," and then waited until they turned their eyes and their attention toward me. "Yesterday you learned that writers write with details." To provide a small example, I added, "Remember how we admired the way that Josh rewrote his first draft, changing 'I gathered my school supplies' so that his next, more detailed version read, 'I zipped my four Bic pens and my puppy-eraser into the pencil case my mother had bought me.'"

Then I said, "Today I want to teach you that writers don't just write with any ol' details, we write with *surprising* details." This sentence, my *teaching point*, ended what I refer to as the Connection phase of the minilesson.

Moving on to what I refer to as the Teaching phase of the minilesson, I said, "Last night, writers, I decided to write a story about my day at the beach. So I wrote, 'We walked across the beach,' and then I thought, 'No, wait. I need to add a detail.' So this time I wrote, 'We walked across the *sandy* beach.' But then I remembered that writers don't just write with any ol' details, we try to write with *surprising* details. And I realized that *most* beaches tend to be sandy, so that's not really a surprising detail. Watch what I did to come up with a surprising detail."

Turning to the white board, I wrote:

We went to the

"Hmm. How shall I describe the beach so my readers can be there with me? Let me picture it in my mind (that's what I often do when I want to come up with a surprising detail). I'm picturing the waves, crashing in, and a stripe of seaweed running down the center of the beach . . . Oh! That's a surprising detail." I added that to my story:

We went to Seapoint Beach. There was a stripe of seaweed down the center of the beach. I stood and watched the waves crash onto the shore.

I ended this component of the minilesson with a little debriefing. "Did you notice that I *almost* wrote, 'I went to the *sandy* beach'? A famous writer, James Merrill, once pointed out that 'the words that come first are anybody's words. We need to make them our own.' Anybody's beach is a sandy one. Did you see that when I made a picture in my mind of exactly what I honestly saw, I came up with a surprising detail,

one that describes not *anybody's* beach but the *particular* beach I visited?"

Shifting into the Active Involvement component of this minilesson, I said, "So let's try writing with surprising details. Pretend you are writing a story about your hand. You write, 'I put my hand in front of me, and I looked at it.' You *could* say, 'I saw five fingers,' but hands *tend* to have five fingers. To write with surprising details, look closely at your hand." I do this. "What *exactly* do you notice? Be honest and precise." I let every one look at his or her hand, mentally reaching for surprising details. "Partner One, write in the air what you might say next in the story." I recited the start of the story: "I put my hand in front of me." Then I looked at my hand, cueing all the Partner Ones to do the same. Finally I mobilized the turn-and-talk: "I saw . . . ."

The room erupted with conversation. For a moment, I crouched among the children, listening to what they were saying. Then I reconvened the class for the final portion of the Active Involvement section of the minilesson. "I heard Sasha say, 'It's got wrinkles? Big ones and small ones? Like a tree.' That's a surprising detail, and it really helps us picture Sasha's hand."

To end the minilesson and Link it with students' ongoing independent work, I repeated the previous day's teaching point as well as that day's, and again mentioned a few of the tips I'd given in the minilesson. "So writers, yesterday you learned that we write with details, and today you learned that writers write not just with any ol' details but with *surprising* details. From this day forward, when you are writing, remember to take the time to picture your subject, and to reach for the surprising details and precise words that will help others picture your subject as well."

COMPONENTS OF A MINILESSON

Let me explain each of the components of the above minilesson in more depth.

Connection

The connection opens the minilesson. Though it is very brief, it is intended to catch children's attention, name the goal of the day, convey how this goal fits with previous work, and ideally, rally children to listen astutely and actively. Usually, it has two main sections. First, we situate today's lesson within the context of previous work, and second, we name the teaching point for the day.

In my example minilesson, the connection is plain, straightforward, and not very developed. I simply repeat the previous day's teaching point—saying something that is probably not new news to anyone: "Yesterday I taught you. . . ." This is a rather common way to start a minilesson, and it is especially appropriate in instances like this one in which the new minilesson extends the previous lesson. There are times when the link between the previous minilesson and the new one needn't be this tight; in those instances it is common for the connection to integrate many lessons that children have learned across a host of previous days or put a new spin on the old work.

One of the most powerful things we can do at the start of a minilesson is to consolidate earlier teaching in an effort to make that work more memorable and more readily useful for children. For example, this series of units begins with a minilesson suggesting that writers can generate ideas for writing by thinking about people who matter to us. The next day's minilesson suggests that writers can generate ideas for writing by thinking not only about *people* but also about *places* that matter to us. By the connection on the fourth day, I say, "So far you've learned that we can generate ideas for writing by thinking of people, places, and *things*

that are important to us." Because many of us are accustomed to the expression *people, places, and things,* this small collection of sources-for-writing-ideas has a catchy quality to it. If day after day I simply listed a hodge-podge of different sources for stories—favorite places, songs we remember, stories that are often retold within the family, memories that are attached to items—that collection of sources would be very hard to recall. It is much easier for children to remember and draw upon the knowledge that writers sometimes think of people, places, or things that matter to us, write one of those down, and then proceed.

Another move I often make during the opening seconds of a minilesson is to refer not to the previous day's minilesson but to work children have done at this same juncture in the writing process during an earlier cycle of writing. For example, when children choose their seed ideas during the essay writing unit, I'm apt to say, "Earlier this year, when you wrote narratives, you learned three strategies for choosing a seed idea. You learned . . . ." Then I go on to teach students ways in which choosing seed ideas for an essay unit is different and the same.

Sometimes during the connection I retell what children learned or did on an earlier day, highlighting a new nuance or aspect of that work. For example, I may have taught several minilessons focusing on strategies children can use to generate ideas for writing; in the connection I might simply mention those strategies and emphasize that as children learn strategies, they are also learning about characteristics of effective topics.

Often one of my goals during this early phase of a minilesson is to make children feel like authors. I may tell how I read their writing the previous night and phoned my sister so I could read her some of the choice parts. I might say that lately it feels as if the class is populated not only by all of them, but also by their wonderful, idiosyncratic characters.

When writing the Connection section of a minilesson, I often summarize previous teaching points. I've learned that it is very important to repeat the exact phrases I used in the previous lesson. If one day I taught the importance of "surprising details," I won't, a day or a month later, rename these as "unusual details," because I know many children will miss the fact that these are two different names for the same thing. If I name one strategy or skill or quality by ten different names, this can confuse children. They end up thinking each name refers to something different yet are unsure of the differences. On the other hand, there are times when I do call something by two interchangeable titles; then I try to use the two terms as synonyms in the same sentence: "When we write narratives, or stories, it is important to remember. . . ."

After the looking-back portion of the connection, I look forward by naming the teaching point for today's minilesson. That is, the teaching point is *not* contained within the Teaching section of the minilesson. After all, the entire minilesson is really an act of teaching.

THE TEACHING POINT After putting our teaching into context, we come straight out and tell children, as clearly as possible, exactly what we want to teach them today. Usually we do this in a sentence, although it may be several sentences. This is the teaching point. Listen to the language of some of my teaching points:

> Today I want to teach you that although there are oodles of things fiction writers can think about as we develop our characters, there are just one or two things that we *must* think about. Specifically, I want to teach you this: every fiction writer needs to know what his or her characters want, what they yearn for, and what gets in the way of their getting what they want.

or

> Today I want to teach you that writers of nonfiction often live like magnets, collecting not only *our* stories but also the *stories of others* (as long as those stories illustrate our main ideas).

or

> Today I want to teach you that in order to learn to "show, not tell," writers often study instances when other authors have done this, and we notice particular strategies those writers have used and think, "I could try that too."

Trying to generalize these teaching points, one probably notices right away that all three begin with the phrase, "Today I want to teach you that. . . ." This exact wording is not crucial in and of itself—what *is* crucial is that the teacher does not say something like this: "Today I want you to make a chart. In the first column list the names of your characters. Beside each name, in the second column, record what that character wants or yearns for. In the third column, record what gets in the character's way of achieving that goal." I am not suggesting that it would necessarily be a bad thing for children to make such a chart—in fact, as I wrote this "bad example" I thought, "Such a chart could conceivably be a helpful one."' What I *am* saying is that minilessons are different from assigned whole-class activities. Minilessons aim to teach skills and strategies that writers use over and over for their own important purposes. Therefore, in a minilesson, instead of saying, "Today I want you to make four columns," we would say, "Today I want to teach you that writers sometimes invent little charts or grids that help us think through a story before we write it. Some writers, for example, find it helpful to make four-column charts."

My point is that in a minilesson, we are teaching a transferable skill that we want our students to draw on as needed from this day forward, throughout their lives. One way to do this is to couch the teaching point inside the phrase, "Today I want to teach you that writers often. . . ."

We must be very explicit in the teaching point. Each of the examples above could have been left vague. I could have said, "Today I want to teach you that although there are oodles of things fiction writers can think about as we develop our characters, there are just one or two things that we *must* think about." Perhaps I could have added, "Today I'll teach you those crucial elements of fiction." But after hearing my teaching point, learners would still not know what I'm trying to teach. My message would have been, "Wait and see." I think learners profit from the sense of control that comes from knowing what they are learning and why they are learning it. So I suggest that teachers come out with it—that we spill the beans—during our teaching point. This means either that we need to be as explicit as possible right off the bat or that it helps to add a second sentence in which we say something like, "More specifically, I want to teach you that . . . ." I tell teachers that the teaching point should be a line or two that a teacher might put onto a class chart and that writers will want to remember always. A teaching point that stops at, "Today I will teach you how to make your characters come to life," is hardly memorable. On the other hand, if that sentence is followed by another—"Specifically I will teach you that in order to bring your characters to life, you need to show them interrelating with each other"—then the teaching point has suddenly become valuable.

Some may ask, "Why is the wording of a teaching point worth fussing about? Is it really a problem if a teacher says, 'Today we will rewrite our leads,' instead of saying, 'Today I will teach you that in order to write an effective lead, it helps to put your character into action, to show what he or she is doing'? Why does the teacher need to frontload the minilesson so that everything is revealed within the teaching point?" And of course it's true that a teacher needn't use a set of specific words in order to teach an effective minilesson.

However, I have found that when we hold ourselves to a teaching point expressed as, "Today I want to teach you that (writers/fiction writers/essayists) often do such-and-such. Specifically, we do this by (a specific strategy)," it is vastly more likely that the minilesson will teach a skill or strategy that children draw on again and again in the future. Minilessons are not a forum for assigning work; they are part of a

workshop in which children make choices about the specific work they will be doing at any one moment. In this context, in which kids are engaged in their own ongoing work, teachers need to focus on giving writers a repertoire of skills and strategies they can draw on as needed. The wording in a teaching point matters because it reveals whether this is a bit of traditional instruction designed to channel students toward a curriculum requirement or it is a minilesson that orients and inspires a writing workshop.

I find that if we don't embed the specifics of what we will teach into the teaching point, we tend to use the Teaching components of our minilessons to tell students these specifics. If my teaching point in the minilesson at the start of this chapter had been, "Today I want to teach you how to select effective details," then later, during the Teaching component, I probably would have said, "Instead of selecting any ol' details, it helps to select surprising details." I might even have given an example of what I meant by a surprising detail. But *telling* is not *teaching*. I would have succeeded in telling children what to do, but I wouldn't have equipped them to do what I talked about.

In the actual minilesson, when it came time for me to teach, I had already told students that surprising details are more effective than any ol' details. Therefore I used the teaching component to demonstrate to students how I come up with those surprising details. I demonstrated the process I use to generate surprising details—a process that involves picturing the scene in my mind, asking, "What *exactly* do I see?" and reaching for the precise words to convey what I imagine.

Let's take an example. I might want to teach students to write more effective lead sentences for their personal narratives. The teacher could say, in the teaching point, "Today I will teach you how to write more effective leads." Such a teaching point would not have a lot of teaching value. Teachers could record it on a chart and repeat it over and over, and kids could learn it by heart, without any benefits at all ensuing! And if the teaching point is so very vague, then chances are good that during the teaching component, the teacher's time will be consumed with giving specifics. Perhaps the teacher would say something like, "To write more effective leads, it often helps to write what the character says or does."

A better option is for that teacher to spill the beans in the teaching point:

> Today I want to teach you that in order to write an effective lead for a narrative, writers often tell what the character says or does. That is, we can write strong leads by starting the story with a bit of dialogue or with a small action.

Then, during the ensuing Teaching component, the teacher will probably demonstrate the processes a writer goes through in order to come up with the dialogue or small action that the writer uses at the start of the story.

Teaching

The Teaching component of a minilesson requires several kinds of planning. We plan how we will teach, we plan the materials we will use, and we plan the content we will teach. Even though this component lasts only about five minutes, that's a lot of planning!

We can use one of several methods within the teaching component. We can demonstrate, we can explicitly tell and give an example, or we can provide scaffolded practice. It is also possible to use inquiry as a teaching method (although the minilessons in this series tend not to do so.) The vast majority of minilessons involve either demonstrating or explicitly telling and providing an example.

Imagine you wanted to teach someone to tie a special kind of knot. If you decided to teach through a demonstration, you'd start at the beginning and go through the process step by step, talking aloud about each step as you progressed. Alternatively, you might decide to explicitly tell how to tie the knot in a little illustrated talk. You'd try to make the talk memorable. You might consolidate all the steps into three main

steps, giving each one a name. Perhaps you'd use a metaphor, as I did when I taught my son to tie his shoes be referring to "bunny-ear loops." Finally, you might want to provide guided practice. "Take hold of the two ends of the ropes," you might say, waiting for your students to do that. "Now...," you'd continue, guiding the learner step by step.

Let's look at each of these methods in more detail.

DEMONSTRATION Using this method involves setting students up to learn from the demonstration; demonstrating step by step, highlighting what you want students to notice; and then debriefing, naming what you hope children learned from the demonstration that might be applicable to another day and another piece.

- Set students up to learn from the demonstration by telling them how you hope they'll watch the demonstration and by naming what you hope they will soon be able to do. You might say, "Pay attention to..." or "Afterward, I'm going to ask you to..." or "Notice how...."

- Demonstrate step by step what it is you hope the writers will soon be able to do. Highlight whatever it is you want writers to notice, sometimes by almost doing the wrong thing and then correcting yourself, sometimes by narrating a specific aspect of your process. Either think aloud or keep up a running commentary—whichever way you choose, reveal what you are doing in such a way that it is replicable.

- Debrief, usually by looking back on what you just did, naming the steps you took.

- Usually take children back to the beginning of the activity or suggest a situation in which they are apt to initiate the activity.

- Either help children practice the same strategy now, or help them recall what they have learned in a manner that sets them up to use this information later.

It is important to set up the demonstration so that students are aware of what you are doing and how they should be watching you. We usually preface our demonstrations by saying something like, "Let me show you how I . . . ." And we often are more specific, adding something like, "Watch and notice how I . . . ."

Here are some specific examples:

Let me show you what I mean. I am going to reread my writer's notebook, looking for an entry that could grow into a whole story. Watch as I read; you'll notice I give each entry a little growing space, a little time to become an idea. I don't just race through entry after entry, saying, "Nope, nope, nope," as I flick past them.

or

Listen while I tell the story "Three Billy Goats Gruff" in a summary way, like a stream of words rushing past me with no rocks to stand on . . . . Now listen as I write in the air a scene from that story. You should be able to hear the difference between a summary, when I am just telling, telling, telling what happened, and a scene, when my characters talk in their character voices and you see what is happening.

A demonstration is a form of procedural or how-to writing. Our purpose is to demonstrate the step-by-step process we used in order to do whatever it is we recommend students do.

In my minilesson about writing with surprising details, for example, I retold the step-by-step processes I had supposedly used the night before in order to write a detail about the beach. I started, as I am apt to do, by creating the context in which I would need to use the technique. I said, "Last night, writers, I decided to write a story about my day at the beach. So I wrote, 'We walked across the beach.'" Then I

demonstrated the step-by-step processes I might go through in order to generate a surprising detail, embedding a few practical how-to tips into this demonstration, ensuring that this portion of the minilesson was instructive. It needed to teach information that was not included in, but was subordinate to, the teaching point. Observe again how I tucked little tips into this small demonstration:

"I thought, 'No, wait. I need to add a detail.' So this time I wrote, 'We walked across the *sandy* beach.' But then I remembered that writers don't just write with any ol' details, we try to write with *surprising* details. And I realized that *most* beaches tend to be sandy, so that's not really a surprising detail. Watch what I did to come up with a surprising detail."

Turning to the white board, I wrote:

We went to the

"Hmm. How shall I describe the beach so my readers can be there with me? Let me picture it in my mind (that's what I often do when I want to come up with a surprising detail). I'm picturing the wave s, crashing in, and a stripe of seaweed running down the center of the beach. . . . Oh! That's a surprising detail." I add that to my story:

We went to Seapoint Beach. There was a stripe of seaweed down the center of the beach. I stood and watched the waves crash onto the shore.

Does this mean that whenever we choose the method of demonstration, we are going to do a bit of public writing in front of the class? No. There are three very common ways we can demonstrate and yet use someone else's writing.

First, we can act out what a famous author probably did. If my teaching point is that writers often start their stories using dialogue, I may use Ezra Jack Keats' book as an example. If I want to teach using demonstration rather than the more obvious choice of explicitly telling and showing an example, I need to fabricate Keats' actions. No problem! I'm apt to say something like this:

> Let me show you how Ezra Jack Keats went about writing the lead to his book, *A Letter to Amy*. I'm pretty sure that he picked up his pencil and thought, "Wait, let me make a movie in my mind of what actually happens." Then in his mind, he made a little scene—almost like a play up on the stage. He put Peter there, sitting at a table, probably, and he said to himself, "What exactly is Peter doing? What's happening?" Pretty soon the idea popped into his head that Peter is muttering to himself and his dog, Willie. Peter says, "I'm writing a letter to Amy." And Ezra wrote that sentence down—see, here it is at the start of his book.

In a similar way, we may demonstrate by reenacting what *a student* did, prefacing this by saying something like: "Watch what Caleb did when he went about writing his lead sentence. He first . . . ."

We may not only demonstrate what a writer did in order to produce a bit of text, we may also demonstrate what *we* do in order to learn from a text. Take the beginning of this day's teaching component:

> Listen to one of the most famous bits of non-narrative writing in the world. You've heard it before—it is Martin Luther King Jr.'s "I have a dream" speech. I think we can benefit from studying the way Martin Luther King Jr. uses lists to support his ideas. I want you to listen first to a bit of his speech and then watch how I, as a writer, go back and study what this author has done in order to borrow his techniques.

At the end of the demonstration, we often review the step-by-step processes we just walked though, extrapolating what we hope children

ascertained. Debriefing my minilesson on surprising details, I added in another bit of advice:

> "Did you notice that I *almost* wrote, 'I went to the sandy beach'? A famous writer, James Merrill, once pointed out that 'the words that come first are anybody's words. We need to make them our own.' Anybody's beach is a sandy one. Did you see that when I made a picture in my mind of exactly what I saw, I came up with a surprising detail, one that describes not *anybody's* beach but the *particular* beach I visited?"

More often, however, debriefing serves simply as a way to consolidate and crystallize whatever it is that we hope students take with them.

EXPLICITLY TELLING AND SHOWING AN EXAMPLE Using this method involves explicitly telling students a concept you hope can guide them today and in the future, then laying out an example that makes this as memorable or as helpful as possible.

- Perhaps begin by describing the context in which today's teaching point will be useful.

- Explicitly tell students a concept you hope can guide them today and in the future. Teach this in a way that makes it as memorable or as helpful as possible. Usually this means telling an anecdote or creating a metaphor or sharing a list—in some way trying to bring home your point—and often it means crystallizing your point in a catchy phrase.

- Show the example, highlighting the aspects that will enable children to produce something similar. One way to highlight what a writer did do is to remind people of the alternative choices a writer could have made. Tuck tips and pointers into this discussion in a manner that is informative for the learner.

- Reiterate what you have taught, often reminding learners of situations in which the concept will be useful.

Although there are advantages to *demonstration* as a method for teaching, sometimes when I want to convey a concept or an idea, I find myself wanting to give students a little talk rather than act something out. I am mindful that if I sit in the front of the class and blab on and on, the chances that my lesson will be memorable are especially weak. Therefore, I regard this method as especially challenging and I work especially hard to get it right.

I essentially use the same techniques to talk to kids that I use when I'm giving a keynote address to teachers. I often rely on a well-told, usually personal story. I may turn a story into a metaphor I hope will convey the concept I'm trying to teach. I often use parallel structure, with repeating phrases.

Some of my favorite minilessons rely on this teaching method. For example, in *Units of Study for Primary Writing*, I tell children that sometimes writers come up with great big watermelon ideas, thinking, "I'll write about my summer," or "I'll write about recess." Then I tell children that writers know that it helps to reach, instead, for a little seed story, writing about tubing down a creek or falling from the monkey bars. Many future minilessons reference this one; later when children write all-about books (or informational books), their job is to select a watermelon topic, and each seed becomes a separate chapter.

Another time, I tell children that revision means quite literally to "see again." Then I say that the one thing they need to revise is—here I reach for my prop—glasses. They are surprised, of course, and I laugh and say they don't really need glasses to revise but they do need

to put on a special lens and reread their writing with that lens. Then I tell them that writers can choose the lens we'll use, but that I especially recommend writers reread their essays with the lens of structure.

I also use the explain-and-give-an-example teaching method in a minilesson in which I invite children to build spaces in their lives that support them as writers. I can't very well create such a space before their eyes, so I rely on storytelling. Early in the minilesson, I say, "Today, I thought I'd tell you that when I begin a new writing project, I do one other very important thing: I clean my office. Many writers take the time to set up spaces in which we can do our best work." Then I tell the story of Annie Dillard, who turned a tool shed into a study, pushing a long desk against a blank wall so that she'd have nowhere to look but onto the page. Then I generalize from this example: "Do you see how Annie Dillard has built a place for her writing, a place that reminds her of what she wants to remember as she writes? She makes sure her place whispers a message to her." And then I name my teaching point: "Today I want to teach you that most writers set up spaces in which we can do our best work as writers, and we put into those spaces items and words that remind us of all we resolve to do and be as writers. Wouldn't it be great if instead of putting up portable classrooms outside this school, they instead put up tool sheds, one for each of us? It'd be great if we could each set up a writing shed for ourselves, but in this classroom we can only set up our writing spaces, our notebooks, our folders. Still, it is important to choose items that we can put near us as we write, items that carry with them bits of advice." Then I tell about how I put things near me as I write that remind me of lessons I've learned earlier and don't want to forget.

Each of these explain-and-give-an-example minilessons are deliberately written in such a way that the message is memorable. I think of these minilessons as little keynote speeches and try to inspire and entertain as well as inform.

GUIDED PRACTICE OR INQUIRY These two teaching methods are less common than explaining and giving an example. Both of them follow a similar sequence:

- Perhaps begin by describing the context in which today's teaching point will be useful.

- Explicitly and briefly tell students a skill or concept you hope to impart. Usually this skill or concept is one that writers use repeatedly in the midst of writing.

- Get them started doing the thing and interject lean prompts to scaffold the child's work. Your scaffolds may help the child progress through a sequence of activities, but they are more likely to ratchet up the level of the child's work.

- Debrief, naming what you have taught and reminding learners of situations in which the skill or concept will be useful.

This method is used fairly often in conferences, less often in minilessons. Rather than demonstrating or talking about what we hope students learn and then stepping back while children have a chance to try the thing we have taught, we sometimes teach by telling very briefly and then giving children scaffolded practice. For example, when I want to teach children to insert periods at the ends of their sentences, I tell them that writers think of a thought, say it in a sentence, write that whole sentence without pausing, and then, when we do pause, we insert a period. Then writers think of the next thought, say that next thought in a sentence, again write that whole sentence without pausing, then pause to think of what comes next, and again record a period. I show this very briefly by dictating a series of sentences to myself and punching the air each time I pause at the end of one. But within a minute or two, I've gestured for the class to join me, and now we are all punching the air whenever we reach the end of a sentence. Then I ask children to continue dictating their thoughts, this time to a partner. As they talk to each other,

I intercede with reminders: "Don't pause till you reach the end of that thought." "Don't forget the period (punch) when you pause."

In the above example, my interjections lift the level of the children's repeated actions. Sometimes, instead, I guide them, step-by-step, through a sequence of work. For example, when children are writing narratives and I want to help them avoid summarizing and instead *tell* the story, I'll walk them though a sequence of prompts. "Think of one particular time when you were doing something," I might say, giving children a moment to settle on one episode. "Now make a movie in your mind of the very start of this. Where were you, exactly? What were you doing, saying? Write this down. Now reread what you've written and in your mind, be there. Put yourselves in the shoes of your character. What happened next—exactly?"

When we use the guided practice method in conjunction with the inquiry method, we are essentially coaching children through the process of learning something about writing for themselves, usually through mentor texts. "Read lots and lots of examples of whatever it is you want to learn or learn from," we say. Then we coach children how to look for patterns in what they've studied, extrapolating rules or techniques to emulate. Then we coach them how to take what they've learned and apply it to their own writing to serve their own purposes.

The Teaching component of a minilesson usually follows the general design of an essay: explicitly and briefly we tell children what we hope they extrapolate from this minilesson, this text; then we show an example or give a demonstration; and finally we reiterate what it is we have told them.

Active Engagement

We learn more from our own actions than from words out of someone else's mouth. Therefore, after we have shown or told or demonstrated a strategy to youngsters, we try to engineer things so that children have a few minutes of scaffolded practice doing whatever they've just learned.

I usually use different texts in the Teaching and Active Engagement components of the minilesson. For example, in the surprising details minilesson, I demonstrated by talking about a story I'd worked on at home about the beach, but when it came time for children to be actively involved, trying the strategy, I didn't ask them to work on my beach story (they didn't have enough information about my day at the beach to do so!). Instead, I set children up by saying, "Pretend you are writing a story about looking at your hand," and got them started practicing the strategy in a miniature, short-term piece about that readily available and universal topic. Both my text about the beach and the text I asked children to use for practice were just "one-day texts." Neither the beach story nor the hand story threads its way through a series of minilessons. Their redeeming feature—and the reason they are used in this minilesson—is that they are instantly accessible. I could speak for just seconds about each story and the children could still grasp my meaning enough to focus on the particular point I was trying to make.

Often, in order to keep the Active Engagements as simple as possible, teachers will return to a text that the children worked with in previous minilessons. For example, throughout the personal essay unit of study, I demonstrate with references to an essay about my father, and children practice by working on a whole-class essay about their shared work with first-grade reading buddies.

Some teachers are surprised that we don't regularly ask children to pull out their own drafts and practice with them. For example, if I reference Keats' *A Letter from Amy* in the minilesson, showing how Keats probably went about imagining a bit of dialogue to use at the start of that story, people are sometimes puzzled that I'm not apt to then say, during the Active Engagement section of the minilesson, "So get out your most recent draft and reread your lead," and then help children get started transferring the lessons from Keats' book to their own writing.

First, asking children to look at their own drafts and either say aloud to a partner or begin incorporating what has just been taught into their own work is indeed an option and teachers may, in their own minilesson, make choices that differ from mine. If your children do not write anywhere near enough during the writing workshop and you want to give them a nudge to get more writing done, you might want them to use the Active Engagement component to get started on their own work. And if you are less concerned that children learn to use strategies with independence and more concerned that they are mobilized to do *something* productive, you might use this section of the minilesson as a time for them to rehearse aloud for the writing you desperately hope they will do that day.

My rationale for often using an "exercise text" rather than having children practice on their own writing is this: if every child essentially accomplishes whatever I have taught within the two-minute Active Engagement component of the minilesson, then when I say, "Off you go," and send children back to their seats, they will have mostly finished their work for the day. Then, too, I want children to become accustomed to initiating the strategies they learn in minilessons, reaching for these strategies only when the moment seems right for this within their own writing process. And although I may take just a few minutes to teach a strategy, I hope that when they incorporate this strategy into their own writing, the work becomes more complex and involved than anything that could fit into a few minutes of work in the midst of the minilesson. For these reasons, I often set children up to be able to work successfully with what is essentially a whole-class text. Because they are all working with the same text for a moment or two, they especially will be able to learn from each other's work.

For example, in my minilesson on writing with surprising details, I set children up to try what I'd taught this way:

> "Did you notice that I *almost* wrote, 'I went to the sandy beach'? A famous writer, James Merrill, once pointed out that 'the words that come first are anybody's words. We need to make them our own.' Anybody's beach is a sandy one. Did you see that when I made a picture in my mind of exactly what I saw, I came up with a surprising detail, one that describes not *anybody's* beach but the *particular* beach I visited?"

We went to Seapoint Beach. There was a stripe of
seaweed down the center of the beach. I stood and
watched the waves crash onto the shore.

"So let's try writing with surprising details. Pretend you are
writing a story about your hand. You write, 'I put my hand
in front of me, and I looked at it.' You *could* say, 'I saw five
fingers,' but hands *tend* to have five fingers. To write with
surprising details, look closely at your hand. What *exactly*
do you notice?"

In this instance, as in many Active Engagements, because the children
are all using a shared text, I am able to set them up and get them started
doing what I want them to do, thereby orienting them to the work and
building their momentum so there isn't a time lag at the beginning. In fact,
I often get children started by joining them in doing the strategy in the way
I suggest. That is, at the start of many Active Engagements, it almost looks
as though this will be another demonstration—and then at the last
moment, I pass the baton to the class. For example, in the minilesson
about the importance of surprising details, I did not launch children in the
Active Engagements component by assigning them to do some work. I did
not say, "So would you examine your partner's hand and notice details,
surprising details. Then tell your partner what it was you saw." Instead I
joined the children in doing this, as if I was running along beside their
bike, building up their momentum before pulling my hands away:

"So let's try writing with surprising details. Pretend you are
writing a story about your hand. You write, 'I put my hand
in front of me, and I looked at it.'" I did this. "You *could*
say, 'I saw five fingers,' but hands *tend* to have five fingers.
To write with surprising details, look closely at your hand."
I do this. "What *exactly* do you notice? Be honest and
precise." I let everyone look at his or her hand, mentally
reaching for surprising details. "Partner One, write in the
air what you might say next in the story." I reread and

enact the start of the story: "I put my hand in front of me."
Then I look at my hand, cueing all the Partner Ones to do
the same. Finally I mobilize the turn-and-talk: 'I saw....'"

Usually the work that we set children up to do during this
component is either "turning and talking" or "writing in the air." The
difference is that the first prompt asks children to discuss, the second
asks one child to dictate to the other what he or she could write. That is,
if I said, "Turn and talk about surprising details you could mention if
you were writing about your hand," I would expect children to say
something like this: "Uh, I don't know. That it's got wrinkles? Big ones
and small ones? Like a tree." Children would speak differently if instead
I had said, "Partner One, write in the air what you might say next in your
story. 'I looked at my hand. I saw....' Turn and write in the air." In that
case the comment would probably be expressed like this: "Wrinkles, big
and small ones, branching out like a tree."

Of course, there are lots of exceptions to what I've said about Active
Engagement. One of the more common ones is that sometimes it is not
easy to set children up to do what we've taught. In these instances, we
sometimes ask children to function as researchers, telling each other
what they saw us (or an author) do. We can also ask children to function
as planners, telling each other what they plan to do. And certainly, there
are times when we want them to get started doing some work on their
own piece during this moment of scaffolded practice.

Usually the Active Engagement component of a minilesson leads up
to some type of closure. If children have been working in pairs, we will
have listened in on that work. The most common way to bring closure is
to say, "I heard you (repeat the teaching point here). Listen to how (refer
to one or two children who did the work well, providing yet more
examples of good practice)." It is crucial, of course, that we don't refer to
the same children over and over. Sometimes the child being spotlighted
did especially strong work only because we were scaffolding his or her
partnership conversation, but when we retell the child's achievements,
we leave ourselves out, giving the child full credit for the effective work.

Link

During this final section of a minilesson, we restate our teaching point and either try to ensure that every child applies this new learning to their ongoing work today or encourage children to add today's teaching point to their repertoire of possible strategies or goals.

Pulitzer Prize–winning writer Donald Murray once told me that the single most important sentence in a paragraph is the last one. "This sentence needs to propel readers onward to the next paragraph. It needs to be not a closing, but a launch." I remember this advice when I reach the final bend in my minilessons. These last few sentences need to encapsulate the content of the minilesson in such a way that kids get their hands around it and carry it with them as they head off into the whole of their writing lives.

The challenge of teaching in a way that makes a real difference is not for the faint of heart. It's a tall order to believe that we can call children together into a huddle and take five minutes to teach a technique and they'll then add that technique to their repertoire, using it when the time is right.

And so we speak with great energy. "And so I'm hoping that today and every day," we say with great solemnity, knowing this repeating phrase may matter more than anything else in our teaching, "you'll take time to reread your work and ask, 'Does this make sense?' If it doesn't make sense, class, what do writers do?" "Fix it!" "That's so smart of you. Thumbs up if you are quite sure that from this day onward, you'll be the kind of writer who rereads your own work and asks, 'Does that make sense?' All of you?! Wow! That is so cool. The writers who are seated at the blue table can get started. At the green table…."

I try to remember four things when I plan the Link between my minilesson and writing time:

- *Crystallize the lesson.* I consolidate the lesson into a clear, even catchy phrase that will be easy for children to hold on to and remember. I may repeat the key phrases several times during the last minute of the minilesson, and I know I'll weave these phrases into future conferences and minilessons. The key phrase in the minilesson might be, "Writers look with honest eyes," or "Remember, you are not just a writer, you are a writing teacher," or "Writers show, not tell," or "Take a small moment and make it big," or "Writers add, and writers subtract," or "Let Eve Bunting be your writing teacher." Whatever it is, I find ways to repeat those words so they become a song in children's minds.

- *Generalize the lesson.* As the day's minilesson ends, I want children to remember that it applies to every day's writing. Sometimes I'll make sure everyone uses the tool that very day, but just as often I'll want children to use the tool only when they need it. Either way, however, I need to remind children that the lesson is for "today, and every day" and that "from this day onward" they'll need to remember this tool. Sometimes it helps to put the lesson onto a chart where it accumulates alongside others and remains visible. Such charts might be titled How Writers Revise; Finding Topics for Writing; When Writers Are Done, They've Just Begun; What Good Writing Teachers Do; Qualities of Good Writing; Lessons Mem Fox Can Teach Us. It is also important that teachers move between specific examples and general principles. If the minilesson has been geared toward teaching one new trick for turning narratives into poems, I'll want to be sure to say, "So you can do any of these things when you want to turn a narrative into a poem," and then I'll reread the whole list, adding the new item.

- *Make the transitions smooth.* It's worth my time to think about how to move my twenty-five kids expediently from the carpet to their workspaces. It's worthwhile to develop and refine a system that will then remain in place almost every day. If the system is always changing, it becomes forefront in children's minds and in our own, and at this crucial juncture, our hope is that children's minds are on their writing topics and plans.

- *Boost the children's writing energy.* Don Murray once said, "Above all, in a writing conference, the writer's energy for writing needs to go up, not down." The same can be said about the Link. Above all, it needs to boost children's energy for writing, not sap it.

Studying the craft of effective minilessons can change our teaching not only in the writing workshop but also in other disciplines, and it can improve not only our whole-class but also our small-group instruction. The power of the template is that it is usable and strong for every kind of teaching, both throughout the school day and throughout our lives and interactions with other learners. Just as a powerful minilesson has a replicable, potent, portable lesson in it, the *template* for a minilesson has those same qualities. It is meant to be a framework that is useful to us forever, in many kinds of situations.

CHAPTER 8

THE PATTERNS OF CONFERENCES

The writing workshop approach to teaching writing is also referred to as the conference approach, because one-to-one conferring is at the heart of this method of teaching. These conferences are essential: when a teacher talks with a child about the child's rough drafts, the child internalizes this conversation and, in the end, is able to talk with himself or herself in the midst of writing. The writing process, in a sense, is an internalized conversation that occurs *within* any skilled writer. The writer digs in to write, then pulls back to reread and rethink, shifting between being passion-hot, and critic-cold, between pouring words onto the page and pausing to ask, "What am I really, *really* trying to say? Does any of this draft capture what I want to say?"

Research on the teaching of writing has shown that if teachers habitually approach children in the midst of writing and ask, "What are you planning to do next with this draft?" or "What do you think is especially strong in this draft that you can build on?" or any similar query, children eventually internalize these questions. The child in the midst of writing, will pause and say, "Let's see, what do I plan to do next with this draft?"

It is tremendously important, then, that we confer regularly with children, and that we do so in ways that teach children to confer with themselves. We need to ask writers the questions that writers can profitably ask themselves. And we need, as much as possible, to hand over the conferences to the children, letting them become, with our support, both writer and reader, creator and critic.

It is no surprise that writing conferences (like minilessons) have a predictable architecture. After we listen in on this conference, I'll show how it typifies many conferences.

A TYPICAL CONFERENCE

I watched Regio rereading his story about playing Frisbee® with his Labrador Retriever. At various points, he paused to insert a word or a phrase into his draft: the color of the dog's collar and the Frisbee®, a description of his lawn—lush and green. "Hi, Regio," I said. "What are you working on as a writer?"

"Frisbee® with my dog," he said.

"You are writing a story about playing Frisbee® with your dog, is that what you mean?" I said. "Huh! That sounds like fun." Then I added, "But Regio, my question is this—what are you working on, that is, what are you trying to do as you write?"

This time Regio responded, "I'm adding details."

"Can you show me?" I said. Soon I'd seen some of Regio's additions. I laughed appreciatively at a description of his dog biting on a Frisbee®, and for a few seconds we commiserated about owning retrievers who never want to stop retrieving. Then, wondering about Regio's rationale for adding the very small details he'd inserted into the draft, I asked, "What led you to add that the dog's collar was blue, and details like that? What specifically were you trying to do with that sort of detail?"

Regio explained that he wanted people to be able to picture it. Listening to him, I worried that he seemed to be reciting someone else's reasons for revising rather than really sharing any special commitment of his own, and I tucked this thought into a corner of my mind.

"What are you planning to do next?" I asked, wondering whether he had some other intentions up his sleeve. I learned that Regio thought he'd add a few similar details; then he figured he'd recopy the piece to make it look better, be able to pronounce it done, and publish it.

"Regio," I said, shifting now into the Compliment stage of this conference, "I'm totally impressed that you've chosen to write about this incident with your dog. You and I are kind of the same because we both have retrievers, and your story has reminded me that I could do the same. I could take just an everyday incident with Toby and try to write it really well—and it would almost be as if I were making a snapshot of Toby, only in words. I'm also impressed that without anyone suggesting it, you went back and reread your draft and added in more details to help readers really imagine your dog. I love that you're in charge of your own writing. You not only choose your own topics, you also go between drafting and revising all on your own. That's very writerly of you!"

"But can I teach you one thing?" I waited for a shrug or a nod. "When writers try to put details into our personal narratives, we add the true details that we really noticed when the event was happening. So if I were going to write about walking into the school's front foyer today, I wouldn't say, 'I walked into the front foyer of the school. I saw that the main office was beside the front foyer'—I've been coming here for years and I no longer notice it's there." But I *might* have said, 'I walked into the front foyer of the school. I noticed that the display case was filled with colorful flags. I looked closer and saw there was a flag from every state.' Do you see how as a writer of a personal narrative, I include the true details that I actually noticed when the event was happening? That allows a reader to read the draft and to picture the true details that stand out in the moment of the story."

"Why don't you try that? Reread your draft, and give each of the details you've included a test. Ask, 'Is it likely that I really noticed this detail at the time the event was occurring?' I'm pretty sure the answer will be no some of the time. You are the kind of writer who revises on your own, so it probably won't be hard for you to do what professional writers do—revise your revisions! Cross them out! Then you can go back and remember exactly what did happen when you and Banjo were playing on the lawn and this time try to add only the details that you would have noticed then." Turning the draft so that Regio could see it, I said, "Get started, reread a bit of your draft aloud while I'm here and give those details a test while I watch. Okay?"

Regio did that, crossing out a few of his details at the top of his page. "You are great at giving these details the Truth Test," I said. "Before you read on, will you try revising not only by subtracting, but also by adding?" I waited and saw him return to the passage he'd just read, rereading it. I murmured, "Smart decision to reread. Make sure you are picturing the True Thing that happened. What exactly did Banjo do?"

"He put the Frisbee between his paws and sorta said, 'You can't have it?'" Regio responded, his inflection rising as if he wasn't at all sure he was on track.

"Oh my gosh, that is *per*fect! Add that!"

THE ARCHITECTURE OF A CONFERENCE

My conference with Regio, like many of my writing conferences, follows a predictable structure. I begin by researching what he is in the midst of doing as a writer and what he intends to do next. I also try to glean what he feels about his draft and his work. I read sections of his draft that he has referenced, glancing over the whole piece. This phase takes a couple of minutes. Sometimes during this phase I look over a larger amount of the student's work.

Then I compliment Regio. I try to compliment something I believe either is a new accomplishment or at least is important to the writer. I try to name what the writer has done in ways that make that work transferable to another piece and another day. Sometimes I try to articulate the steps the writer probably went through to accomplish the thing I'm complimenting, making it likely that the writer will do similar work another time. Often I hope that my compliment will support a child's identity as a writer and/or the child's commitment to this writing project.

Then I name what I want to teach as explicitly as possible, again making sure that my teaching point will be transferable to another piece and another day, and teach it. Sometimes my teaching in a conference involves demonstrating; if so, I do this much as I might in a minilesson. Fairly often I ask a writer to get started doing the new work, as I did with

Regio, and I coach or otherwise support the writer's beginning efforts. Before my time with the writer is over (either that day or later) I try to extrapolate from this one episode some enduring lessons that I hope the writer has learned.

Let's look more closely at each of these components of an effective conference.

The Research Phase

In my conference with Regio, as in almost every conference, I begin with Research. Often my research starts with a bit of observation. From afar, I check out what various writers are doing, and muse over possible ways I might contribute. Often, it is only after I have a hunch about ways that I might help that I pull my chair close to a particular writer and begin to ask questions.

I ask Regio the one question I ask over and over during this phase of a conference: "What are you working on as a writer?" Because I ask this same question often, I make sure that children learn how to answer. I am not surprised when Regio responds by telling me his topic—this is what most writers do until we teach them otherwise. So when Regio says he is working on "Frisbee® with my dog," I let him know I've heard him—"You are writing a story about playing Frisbee® with your dog, is that what you mean?"—but then I clarify that my question has not actually been, "What are you *writing about*?" I say, "But Regio, my question is this—what are you working on, that is, what are you trying to do as you write?" This time Regio points out, "I'm adding details."

If Regio had struggled with that question, as children often do at first, I would have provided more support by turning it into multiple choice. Either using the chart of recent teaching points or glancing at his writing as a reference, I would have said, "Are you trying to make sure your characters come to life, or are you working on writing with details, or are you trying to make sure you write in paragraphs, or what?" giving Regio the idea for the sort of response I expect.

Because I don't want simply to draw children toward my own

assessments and plans for their writing, I think it is important to begin a conference by learning about the writer's intentions. For this reason, "What are you working on as a writer?" is an incredibly common question, although there are other ways to word essentially the same request for information. And because the question matters, we teach children how to respond to the question. That is, we teach them that we want to learn not just about their content ("playing Frisbee® with my dog") and not just about their genre ("a personal narrative about playing with my dog") but also about their goals and strategies ("I'm writing a personal narrative about playing Frisbee® with my dog and I am trying to write with a lot of details").

If a number of children in a particular class are struggling with the "What are you working on as a writer?" question, I am apt to stop the class and talk to all the children about the importance of having goals and strategies. I teach children the sort of goals and strategies I expect they might have, and ask them to assign themselves one at the start of their work by taking stock of where they are in the writing process and choosing their next step.

Once Regio tells me that he has been working on adding details, it is clear I need to study those efforts. "Can you show me?" I ask and soon see (and build some theories about) some of Regio's additions. I theorize that he doesn't feel especially committed to his revisions or to the writing itself, and I speculate that he is trying to add sensory details as a paper-and-pencil endeavor, simply inserting color words here and there without really envisioning his subject—his dog—at all. I want to check *his* rationale for adding these particular details, however, so I ask, "What led you to add that the dog's collar was blue, and details like that? What specifically were you trying to do with that sort of detail?" His answer confirms my hypothesis, as do his answers about his future plans for the piece.

The work I do during the Research component of this conference is fairly typical. The writer conveys the aspect of writing that has occupied

his or her attention, and the teacher tries to understand the writer's knowledge, intentions, assessments, and plans pertaining to that aspect of writing. This almost always involves probing to understand what the child means. Regio tells me that he has been trying to add details. Of course I know what it means to add details to a piece—but I don't know what this means for this nine-year-old! I could have asked any of these questions at this point: "What kind of details do you think are important?" "Do you just add details all over the draft or do you add them in particular places?" "Why did you choose these particular details to add?" The point of these questions is that we, as teachers, need to understand the writer's understanding. Often children will throw terms around, saying back whatever words we have said to them, and we need to get below the glib phrases and really understand the writer's concepts of revision and of good writing.

Especially when I don't feel that the area the child is focusing on merits more of the child's attention, I am apt to probe a bit to see whether the writer has any other plans up his or her sleeve. (Of course, I let the draft inform me as well.)

Usually when I try to help graduate students learn to confer well, I find that the source of most of their troubles lies in their research. They don't spend enough time trying to understand what the writer is doing and why. As a result, what they decide to teach is often an utterly generic point, perhaps just a recap of a minilesson. That is, when a conference doesn't begin with a teacher really taking into account what the child has done and is trying to do, then during the Teaching section of the conference, the teacher seems to be reciting canned material unaffected by this particular student and his or her work. Our conferences can be among the greatest sources of originality and new thinking in our teaching but only if they are truly responsive. The vitality and originality that characterize really powerful conferences require that we, as teachers, take in what the writer is doing, planning, working to achieve, understanding, and knowing. My first book was titled *Lessons from a Child*, and I continue to believe that conferences give us the chance to learn from the only people who can really teach us how to teach!

Sometimes I help teachers understand the importance of this Research phase by asking them to think about times when a principal has observed their teaching. How helpful it is if the person who coaches us first listens and observes to learn what we are already trying to do! One teacher I know always worries about the strugglers in her classroom. Realizing this, she set herself a correction course, deliberately focusing on her strongest students for a week or two. Her principal sat in on a few moments of her teaching and then told her that she mustn't focus so much on her strong students! If that administrator had prefaced the visit by asking, "What have you been working on? How's it been going?" the coaching interventions could have been far more helpful.

The Decision Phase

To an outside observer, a conference may seem fairly relaxed. But for me, as a teacher, conferences are anything but. As the young writer talks and as my eyes quickly take in the draft and any other available data, my mind is always in high gear. Malcolm Gladwell, the author of the bestselling book *Blink: The Power of Thinking Without Thinking*, suggests that he can observe a married couple for just half an hour and predict the chances that their marriage will be intact a decade hence. In a conference, I'm trying to do an equally astonishing feat of "thin-slicing." I take in all the data I can quickly assimilate, and as I do, I'm theorizing, predicting, connecting this writer to other writers I've known, determining priorities, imagining alternate ways to respond, and lesson planning! All this must happen while I smile genially and act captivated enough by what the child says to keep the data coming my way! This is no easy task, and teachers are wise to recognize that this invisible aspect of teaching writing is the most challenging one of all.

In the Deciding phase of a conference (which in actuality happens simultaneously with the Research as well as in the handful of seconds between the Research and the Compliment), I quickly synthesize what I have learned and imagine possible paths to take that will best help the writer.

It is important to note that I deliberately delay acting on what I have learned until I have made a conscious decision. That is, I take in whatever I can and then say to myself, "Hmm," being very careful, at all costs, not to slip unconsciously between researching, complimenting, and teaching. Instead I hope that it will always be crystal clear to me, to the student, and to any observer when I move from researching to complimenting to teaching.

During the Decision phase, I am deciding at least two things: what to compliment and what to teach. In making this decision, I draw on these considerations.

- If possible, I equip writers to do what it is they intend to do. When I ask, "What are you working on as a writer?" and "What are you trying to do with this piece?" my purpose is to learn the writer's intentions so that I can support and extend what the writer is already trying to do (if that seems fruitful) and equip the writer with more (or better) strategies for achieving his or her intentions. That is, I do not want my interactions with children inadvertently to teach them they might as well not have any plans or intentions for their own writing, because when they bring their writing to me, I will always come up with a direction they could not possibly have imagined. Instead, I want children to feel as if they have some ownership over their writing, that their hands are on the steering wheel. Given that there are usually lots of ways children could improve their drafts, I will, whenever possible, align my teaching with their own plans and intentions.

- On the other hand, there are times when I think the writer's intentions are too constricted or are otherwise ill advised. When I don't want to get behind the child's existing intentions (or can't discern what they are), I first try to rally the child to take on a new intention. For example, if a child is writing in bare outlines but only wants help with spelling, one alternative is slyly to elicit details and get the child to record them. This would accomplish the goal of making the text more detailed, but it would not make a lasting impact on the writer. I am more apt, therefore, to talk to the writer about his or her goals, encourage him or her to see the importance of writing with detail or some other goal I've chosen based on my assessment, and then briefly talk up the overall direction and goals I'm advocating, before equipping the child to pursue those goals.

- I'm always teaching toward independence and growth. I try to decide on an intervention that will extend what children can already do but also to teach within their reach so that what they do with my support today, they can do independently tomorrow. This means that I sometimes act very excited about a goal that is not really an end goal but a halfway goal. I'll teach a child to add details and watch as the child rereads, using a carrot to add details that fit into a few phrases; while I well know that my real goal is for the child to write details that span paragraphs, I meanwhile act very pleased over what he or she has done.

- I am always informed by my goals. These goals come

from an overall sense of what I value in young writers (the ability to write well-structured stories, a growing control of conventions, a readiness to emulate other authors, and so on) and what I value in learners (initiative, zeal, skills, a willingness to take risks and work hard, self-awareness, a commitment to social justice, and so on), as well as from the specific goals I have in mind for a particular unit of study and a particular child.

The Compliment Phase

When I listen to children talk and look over their writing, the first big question I ask and the first big decision I make revolves around the Compliment. That is, I am thinking first, "What has the child done—or gestured toward doing—that I could name and make a fuss over?" Either at the end of the Research/Decision phase or earlier, I spot something that the child has done (or has almost done) that has significance in the child's learning journey, and I name this in a way I hope makes it likely that the child will do this same wise work again in future pieces of writing.

The trick is I need to be able to extrapolate something transferable out of the details of the child's work. If the child added the sound her guinea pig makes when it squeaks into her draft, I don't say, "I love that you added the *ee, ee, ee* sound to your story. I hope you add that squeaking sound into your stories often!" Instead, I name what the child has done in a way that makes the action replicable: "I love the way you reread and added teeny details that could help readers create movies in their minds of exactly what happened. You made it so I can picture your guinea pig. Whenever you write, add details like these." Or, "I love the way you've brought out dialogue—even if it is guinea pig dialogue! You didn't just say, 'Freddy made noises to greet me,' you told us exactly what he said!"

After researching to learn what Regio is doing and trying to do and after deciding on my plan for the conference, I say, "Regio, I'm totally impressed that you've chosen to write about this incident with your dog. You and I are kind of the same because we both have retrievers, and your story has reminded me that I could do the same: I could take just an everyday incident with Toby and try to write it really well—and it would almost be as if I were making a snapshot of Toby, only in words. I'm also impressed that without anyone suggesting it, you went back and reread your draft and added in more details to help readers really imagine your dog. I love that you're in charge of your own writing. You not only choose your own topics, you also go between drafting and revising all on your own. That's very writerly of you!"

The truth is, of course, that Regio's revisions don't amount to much. It isn't especially valuable to insert the color of the dog's collar into the draft! And so it takes some discipline for me to see that there is something commendable about his teeny-tiny additions. But I'm glad that I force myself to get behind something Regio has done, because in fact it *is* impressive that he shifts from writing to rereading and revising and does this on his own. And I'm glad that my plan to begin a conference by making a fuss over something good that the writer has done channels my attention in such a way that I see that Regio's work merits support.

As I look for what I will compliment, I am usually thinking, "What has the child done—or gestured toward doing—that represents the outer edge of the child's development and therefore would be something wise for me to extol?" I always want to name what the child has done in such a way that this is exportable to other pieces and other days, and this means extrapolating something transferable out of the details of the child's work.

Often I am getting behind something that the child may have done almost accidentally, and so I try to reiterate the process the child may have taken in order to accomplish the commendable activity. "I can tell that you . . ." I say, naming the step-by-step strategies the child may or

may not have taken. This way, I leave a pathway for the child to repeat his or her accomplishments another time.

The Teaching Phase

The Teaching phase of a conference is remarkably similar to a minilesson. I try to make it very clear that the conference has turned a corner and that I now want to explicitly teach the writer something that I hope will help him, not only today, with this piece, but also in the future. I'm apt to preface this component by saying something like, "But can I give you one tip, one very important tip, that I think will help you not only with this piece but also with future pieces?" Alternatively, I might say, "Can I teach you one thing that I think will really, really help you a lot?" Or, "One thing that I do when I want to (I repeat the writer's goal—convince my reader, write a really effective list, angle a story so that it makes my point) is that I. . . ." This prelude essentially sets me up to make a teaching point.

For example, in my conference with Regio, after complimenting him, I round the bend in the conference like this: "But can I teach you one thing? When writers try to put details into our personal narratives, we add the true details that we really noticed when the event was actually happening." I have carefully worded my teaching point so that I am giving Regio advice that will help not only today with this piece of writing but also other days, with other pieces of writing.

Yesterday, I conferred with half a dozen children who were in the midst of writing essays. These were two of my teaching points:

> "Daniel, what I do after I've written a story that I hope supports the point of my essay is this: I reread my story, chunk by chunk. And after I read each chunk of it, I say to myself, 'Does this part support my topic sentence, yes or no?' Then I go on to the end of the next chunk of text, and I ask that same question."

> "Cassie, after I've collected a few stories that I hope will support my topic sentences, I pause to reread what I've

gathered, and I sort of check over what I've done. I look to see if the stories I've collected really make the point I want to make."

Sometimes I am confident that after making my point, I can ask the writer to go off on his or her own and try the strategy I've just described. Sometimes I feel as if I need to give an example from my own work or even show the writer what this might mean if I were to start doing this sort of work with the writer's text. For example, after telling Regio, "When writers try to put details into our personal narratives, we add the true details that we really noticed when the event was actually happening," I am pretty sure I need to provide an example. So I say, "If I were going to write about walking into the school's front foyer today, I wouldn't say, 'I walked into the front foyer of the school. I saw that the main office was beside the front foyer.'" I explain why—I've been coming to the school for years and therefore I wouldn't be apt to notice the office. Wanting to contrast what I wouldn't do with a positive example of the sort of detail I hope Regio may learn to insert, I say, "I *might* have said, 'I walked into the front foyer of school. I noticed that the display case was filled with colorful flags. I looked closer and saw there was a flag from every state.'"

In Daniel's case, instead of bringing my own case in point to bear, I suggest we reread the first chunk of his story and work together to give it the test of, "Does this support your main idea?" The first chunk does, the second doesn't, and at that point I show Daniel how he can rewrite that episode so that it makes the point he wants to make.

I always begin the Teaching component by explicitly naming something I believe will help the writer not only with this piece but with many pieces. I usually word the teaching point in such a way that it can be generalized to other instances. For example, I might say, "When I am trying to (do what I see you trying to do), I find it is helpful to (progress step-by-step through a replicable strategy)." Of course, this can be worded differently to reference other writers rather than me: "Many writers find that in order to . . . . it helps to . . . . Specifically, they often . . . ."

After this, I decide whether or not the writer needs more detailed help. If yes, I might provide an example or do a demonstration by referring to my own writing or telling a story about another writer. Either way, I generally detail the step-by-step process that a writer goes through and then, often, summarize (still through a sequence of steps) the strategy.

Sometimes I decide to provide even more support by showing writers the sort of thing they might do with their own draft. For example, if the writer has summarized the events that occurred when he went to the airport to pick up his grandmother, saying, "We went and got her at the airport. It was great to see her. We were happy to see her. We took her to her room in my house," I might say, "This would be better if you tell it step-by-step. For example, I could imagine you might rewrite your story so that it went something like this: 'We walked in the big doors at the airport. The air was cold inside. We looked on the wall chart to see where her plane would arrive. "Gate 16," my Dad said. Then we turned to walk toward . . . .'" At this point, I'd say, "I probably didn't get it just right. Can you tell it the true way? Start 'we walked in the big doors . . . .'"

One way or another, I name a teaching point and provide as much support for that teaching point as I think is necessary. If I decide the writer needs more support, I might say, "So let's try this together" then read aloud the relevant portion of the writer's draft or otherwise set the writer up to get started doing the strategy. But, I might simply say, "So would you go off and try this? I think it will work for you this time. And any other time when you are (repeat the situation), remember this is a strategy that you can call on."

When I wanted Regio to reconsider the details he was inserting into his story of playing Frisbee® with his dog, I got him started by saying, "Why don't you try that?" Then I reiterated the sequence of activities. "Reread your draft, and give each of the details you've included a test. Ask, 'Is it likely that I really noticed this detail at the time the event was occurring?'" I anticipated his response and set him up to go farther on his own: "I'm pretty sure the answer will be no some of the time. You are the kind of writer who revises on your own, so it probably won't be hard for you to do what professional writers do—revise your revisions! Cross them out! Then you can go back and remember exactly what did happen when you and Banjo were playing on the lawn and this time try to only add the details that were true then." Turning the draft so that Regio could see it, I said, "Get started, reread a bit of your draft aloud while I'm here and give those details a test while I watch. Okay?"

As writers progress, I provide more or less supportive scaffolds. For example, if the writer is learning to tell a story through a sequence of small steps and needs very strong scaffolds, I can ask, "What did you do first? Exactly what did you say? And then what did you do?" After a few such questions, I can synthesize all that the child has said up to that point and then add one more extending question. But at some point, I need to withdraw some of these very heavy scaffolds so that the child moves toward independence. "Keep going," I soon say. Within another moment or two, my interventions may be just a supportive nod or hand gesture conveying, "Continue. Keep the story rolling."

After Regio crossed out a few of his details at the top of his page, I set him up for the next step by supporting what he'd done and naming what he needed to do:

> "You are great at giving these details the Truth Test," I said. "Before you read on, will you try revising not only by subtracting, but also by adding?" I waited and saw him return to the passage he'd just read, rereading it. I murmur, "Smart decision to reread. Make sure you are picturing the True Thing that happened. What *exactly* did Banjo do?"

> "He put the Frisbee® between his paws and sorta said, 'You can't have it?'" Regio responded, his inflection rising as if he wasn't at all sure he was on track.

> "Oh my gosh, that is perfect! Add that!"

Once the writer has done some work on her or his own (even if that work occurs in the conference, with the benefit of the teacher's scaffolding), it's important to step back and name what the writer has done that we hope the writer does again in another instance within this draft or when working on another piece of writing. In a sense, the conference ends with a second Compliment, one not unlike the first. This second compliment functions rather as the Link does in a minilesson. Usually I repeat the teaching point, this time not as a charge to the writer but as a record of what the writer has just done. These compliments are not unimportant. The single most important guideline to keep in mind in a conference is this: "The writer should leave wanting to write."

And so my conference with Regio ended, "What you are doing is brilliant, Regio. From now on, always remember that you are the kind of professional writer who not only writes but also rereads your writing. When you reread your writing, you pay attention to your details. You give them the Truth Test, don't you? You ask, 'Is this a true detail, one I would actually have noticed when the event was occurring?' And if the detail isn't true, you cross it out and add ones like you just did that are exactly true details.'"

When we follow the general pattern outlined above, conferences become more manageable. In a one-hour writing workshop, having half a dozen intense, meaningful teaching interactions, each one tailored to the individual needs of a child, is difficult enough. Reinventing the structure for each conference along the way would be virtually impossible. A general template allows us to channel our attention and our thoughts to the specific next steps each child can take in her growth as a writer, and to think "Out of all the options available to me, what can I teach that might make the biggest difference?"

CHAPTER 9

AUTHORING YOUR OWN UNITS OF STUDY

This series will have done its job well if it not only helps you to *teach the units* described to good effect, but if it also encourages you to work collaboratively with your colleagues to *author your own units of study*. My hope is that you and your colleagues will notice gaps in the yearlong curriculum that my colleagues and I have laid out, and that you will decide to work collaboratively to create units of study to fill those gaps. Better yet, I hope that teachers at one school (or one grade level) become especially knowledgeable about one facet of a writing curriculum, and teachers at another school (or grade level) become adept in a different area. Perhaps towards the spring of the year, before teachers across different grade levels meet to compose a curricular calendar for the upcoming year, there could be a gigantic conference with teachers sharing the units of study you've authored. Of course, the units will always need to be labeled "Under Construction."

In this chapter, I will turn the process of creating a unit of study inside-out, sharing the interior work.

DECIDE ON THE SUBJECT FOR YOUR UNIT OF STUDY

First, of course, you will need to decide on what it is you will teach. The units that I've detailed in this series may lead you to imagine that most units of study are genre-based. Certainly there are many genres that I have not tackled in this series and that merit study. For example, you may decide to teach a unit on news stories or feature articles, editorials or investigative reports. Alternatively, you may decide to develop a unit on narrative (or literary) nonfiction—children could study narrative nonfiction writing that chronicles a writer's process of investigating a subject. Then, too, once your children have written realistic fiction, you may decide to teach them historical fiction, science fiction or fantasy.

On the other hand, it is important for you to understand that units of study need not be based on a genre. You could instead teach a unit on aspects of the writing process—certainly many people teach units on revision, for example. You might begin such a unit by suggesting children identify three or four pieces they've written that they believe are "good enough" to merit revision, and then you could teach strategies of revision, supporting children in using those strategies on their portfolio of selected texts.

Alternatively, you could teach a unit focusing on a quality of good writing. For example, you could rally children to closely study places where authors "show-don't-tell." Children could find instances where writers show instead of telling within published texts, revise their existing texts so as to do this more, then draft new texts in which they use all they've learned from studying mentors and revising their own texts. There are other aspects of good writing I could imagine studying: characterization, for example, or the development of setting.

Then, too, you could study a social structure that supports writing. For example, you could design a unit of study called "Writing Friendships," in which you help children consider how to work well with a partner and perhaps with a writing club. How might a writing partnership best help us with rehearsal for writing? With drafting? With revision?

Revision of *teaching* is as essential as revision of *writing*, and front-end revision of teaching, like of writing, is especially efficient. Guard against seizing on the first topic of study that comes to mind and plunging forward. For example, if you and your colleagues see that there is no unit of study on poetry in this series, and decide to develop such a unit for your classroom, that could be a wise decision. But poetry is

surely something you will want children to study again and again across their school career. Perhaps you'd like each year's work with poetry to take on a different focus so that children perceive each year as new, and come to each study with fresh enthusiasm. If you and your colleagues decide to differentiate your poetry units so that you create a spiraling curriculum, you'll want to imagine and create a gradient of difficulty for studying poetry. What might be more accessible for younger writers? More demanding for older writers? Perhaps, for example, you will decide the third grade unit on poetry could highlight reading-writing connections and revision. Perhaps the fourth grade study could focus on language and imagery. Fifth graders, then, could study ways in which poems are metaphoric, noticing that even a poet's use of white space matters, for the poet lays words on a page in a manner that conveys the poet's meaning.

You may wonder whether some topics are more worthy of study than others, and whether there are predictable traps to avoid when selecting a topic for study. These are great questions to ask!

When you decide upon a unit of study, you are taking it upon yourself to channel the young people in your care to devote an entire month of their writing lives toward the subject you settle upon. It goes without saying, therefore, that you need to believe any unit of study you teach (any unit you impose upon your children) must be incredibly important. When a teacher suggests she may want to teach a unit on sea shanties, alphabet books or limericks, for example, I sometimes question whether those areas of study are the most important ways for children to invest their time. Sometimes the rationale for a writing unit is that the choice aligns to a reading or social studies unit. My response to that is that when we design units of study for a writing curriculum, I think we need to keep in mind that our choice should come from our sense of what children need *as writers*; I don't think the goal of aligning disparate subjects should take priority over other goals.

That is, the reason to select one unit of study over another may not be immediately obvious to an outsider. The guiding question for choosing a topic for a unit of study should, I believe, be this: "What writing work will be especially helpful for these kids?" That is, a unit of study contains a line of minilessons on a topic, yes, but it is far more important to realize that a unit of study comprises a month of writing work for the children in our care. Would it be especially beneficial for them to work on writing lots of short texts, whipping through a quick version of the writing process many times? If so, then a unit on poetry might be an option, or a unit on revision, or a unit on writing to make real world difference. Perhaps a teacher decides that she wants her children to become more skilled at writing proficient, first-draft writing on demand—for this reason, she may decide to turn the classroom into a newsroom and teach children to write news articles and editorials.

Here is a final word about one's choice of a unit: The other deciding factor is you. If you are learning to play the guitar and find yourself dying for the chance to dig into song-writing, then consider bringing that passion into the classroom. If you loved your fiction unit and yearn to do more, consider a unit on revision, or on character development (which could invite children to revise several earlier pieces so as to bring the characters to life more)or historic fiction. In the end, children can grow as writers within any unit of study. And whether you are teaching a unit on independence in the writing workshop or on writing to change the world, you need only remember that you are teaching children, and teaching writing. The rest is negotiable.

PLAN THE WORK CHILDREN WILL DO

It is tempting to start planning a unit of study by writing a minilesson for day one and then for day two. What I have found is that if I proceed in that manner, chances are great that those intricate, time-consuming plans will end up being jettisoned.

I'd recommend instead that you begin by thinking about the work that you envision your children will be doing in this unit. For example,

when I was working on the first unit of study in this series, before I could imagine the unit's flow, I needed to decide whether I would be channeling children toward writing one narrative during that month, or two, or several. Also, I needed to decide whether I imagined that the writers would proceed in synchronization with each other, or would some children write three stories and some one? Then, too, I needed to decide whether I imagined that children would progress quickly through rehearsal, spending more time on revision or vice versa?

Before you begin to think about the progression of your minilessons, then, you need to imagine different ways that the unit of study you've selected could proceed, and then weigh the pros and cons of those various alternatives. You won't, of course, be sure how long any stage will take, but you can and must approach a unit of study with some tentative plans.

If your children are fairly inexperienced as writers, then you will be more apt to keep them in synchronicity with each other and more apt to expect them to complete several pieces of writing. It is not an accident that the unit in this series that gives children the most latitude in pacing themselves and the most latitude in designing their own projects is the last unit.

As you plan the work that your children will do within the unit, keep in mind a few ways upper-grade writing units unfold. You might, of course, invent something altogether different, but these are a few common templates for a unit of study:

- Your children might generate lots of one kind of writing, perhaps taking each bit of writing through a somewhat limited amount of revision. Then your children could look back over all of it to choose one piece (presumably from the writing they've only lightly revised) to delve into with more depth, bringing it to completion.

- Your children may each work on one writing project that contains lots of parts or steps, with children working roughly in sync with each other, spending a set amount of time on each step (or aspect) of the piece.

Let's imagine that you decide to teach a unit on poetry. You'd probably find this fits best into the first template. Presumably, at the start of the unit, each child could write and lightly revise a bunch of poems. Then writers could commit themselves to taking one poem (or a collection of poems that address one topic) through more extensive revision and editing. A unit of study on news articles could fit into that same template. News stories are written quickly, so children could generate many of these at the start of the unit, bringing more and more knowledge to them as they learn more. Then you could explain that sometimes a writer decides to extend the news article into a more developed sort of writing, and you could teach children to rewrite one of their articles into an investigative report or an editorial (either project would require more research and revision).

On the other hand, you might decide that within one unit, children will work on a single, large writing project: say, a piece of literary non-fiction, perhaps one requiring research. Perhaps for this unit each child will investigate a different endangered species. You may decide that the first half of the unit will focus not on drafting informational writing but on note-taking. Then, during the second half of the unit, children could draft their literary nonfiction.

Before I write a single minilesson, I bring out a blank calendar for the unit to plan how the children's work is apt to unfold across the month. I imagine that for the first week or week-and-a-half in a unit, children will gather entries—so I mark those days onto the calendar. I do not yet know the specific minilessons I will teach, but I do know the broad picture of what children will be doing during those days. Proceeding in a similar fashion, I mark off the bends in the road of a unit. Even after this, however, I'm not ready to write minilessons.

GATHER AND STUDY TEXTS FOR CHILDREN TO EMULATE

You will need lots of examples of the sort of text you hope your children will write. That is, if you decide to teach a unit on writing descriptively and to emphasize the importance of developing the setting, you'll want to turn your classroom library upside-down looking for examples of the sort of thing you plan to teach. You'll become a magnet for this sort of writing and find examples of it throughout your life. You will very likely want to invite your children to join you in this, depending on where they are in their writing and reading lives at the time.

Soon you will have gathered a pile of writing, and you can begin to sift and sort through it, thinking:

- What are the different categories of texts here?

- What are the defining features of this sort of writing?

- Which of these texts could become exemplars for the unit of study?

In order to make these decisions, you'll need to think not only about the texts but also about your kids. You will want to aim toward goals which are achievable for them. You may well choose texts to serve as exemplars that are not the texts that you, personally, would choose to emulate if you were teaching this unit to a group of adults!

In order to decide upon the texts that you will use as exemplars for the unit, you'll need to take into consideration the particular focus you will bring to this unit. For example, when I taught children to write fiction, I knew that I wanted their stories to be simple, involving just two or three characters and just two or three small moments. I knew, also, that I wanted them to write realistic fiction. Fiction, meanwhile, comes in all shapes and sizes—so I needed to do some research before settling upon "Spaghetti" and *Stevie*, *Fireflies!* and *Peter's Chair*.

Often, you will decide to use your own writing as one touchstone text for the class, and you might also decide to use writing done by another child another year. These are perfectly reasonable choices. You probably won't rely exclusively on any one text, however. Each will have its benefits, and children will profit from studying a variety of texts. Usually in a unit of study, children will work collaboratively to write one shared class text. In the essay unit, for example, I began with an essay about my father, and meanwhile, during the Active Engagement section of many minilessons, children worked in pairs to write-in-the-air a class essay, "Working with Reading Buddies." Before you begin a unit of study, then, you may want to consider not only whether you want to thread an exemplar text through the unit, but also whether kids will work collaboratively on creating a class text.

or revise it in exactly the same ways that you suggest your kids try.

As you read and write, try to think about ways in which the current unit of study could build on previous learning. Not everything that you and your kids do in this unit can be brand new. What is it that kids already know that they can call upon within this unit? What will the new work be?

Think, also, about what is essential in the unit and what is detail. The answer to that question lies not only in the unit itself, but in your hopes for how this unit of study will help your kids develop as writers. If you are teaching poetry with a hope that this will lead children toward being able to engage in much more extensive revision, then this goal influences your decision about what is essential in the unit.

READ, WRITE, AND STUDY WHAT YOU WILL TEACH

I describe units as if they are courses of study for children, and of course the truth is they are courses also for us! In addition to collecting examples of the sort of writing you'll be asking kids to do, you will also want to scoop up all the professional books and articles you can find pertaining to your unit of study. You can learn a lot from books for adult writers, so don't limit yourself to books by and for teachers.

I cannot stress enough that you need to do the writing that you are asking your kids to do. You needn't devote a lot of time to this. The writing that you use as an exemplar text needs to be very brief anyhow, so even ten minutes of writing, four times a week, will give you tons of material to bring into your minilessons. The important thing is that during those ten minutes you work in very strategic ways. Usually you'll begin with a bare-bones, little text, and you'll develop

OUTLINE A SEQUENCE OF TEACHING POINTS

After all this preparation, it will finally be time to outline a sequence of teaching points. When I do this, I am usually not totally sure which teaching points will become minilessons and which will become mid-workshop teaching points or share sessions. Those decisions often come very late, as I revise my unit.

I make my plans within general time constraints. That is, I might say to myself, "I will use about three days for teaching kids to live like poets, generating entries which could become poems." I approach a set of days, then, feeling sure about the most important skills that I want to teach, and the most important content I want to convey. I might approach a poetry unit by saying to myself, "Everyone thinks of poetry in terms of pretty words. I want to emphasize, instead, that poets see the world with fresh eyes, reaching for honest and precise words." If this was my goal, I would try to be clear to myself what it is that I hope kids will know and be able to do after this work.

Before I can write minilessons, I need to set the goals that I will work toward in each part of a unit. I also need to name or invent some practical, expendable, how-to procedures that I believe these young writers can use to achieve the goals. For example, although I will be convinced that it is important for a writer to know how to show-not-tell, I will be less sure which step-by-step procedures, which strategies, will help each particular youngster do this. For this reason, I tend to teach by saying, "One strategy that some writers find helpful is . . ." or "One strategy that you might try is . . . ." Those strategies are expendable.

Whenever we teach anything worth teaching, we need to anticipate that kids will encounter trouble. When I teach kids ways to use mini-stories in their essays, for example, I need to anticipate that this will pose difficulties for some kids. At least half our teaching does not involve laying out brand new challenges but instead involves coaching and supporting kids through predictable challenges.

When we plan a unit of study, it is important to anticipate the difficulties kids will encounter in the unit. We'll want to plan to provide them with the scaffolding necessary to have success with first a pared-down version of what we are teaching and, eventually, with higher level work. For example, I was pretty sure I would need to provide some scaffolding for kids when I taught them that they could reread an essay as from a plane, looking down at the structure, the overall chunks of text. When I told kids to look at the patterns of chunks and think, "What was the author doing in this chunk of text?" and "What about in this one?" I knew that some children would find this confusing. To scaffold children's efforts to do this, I boxed out the major sections of a text I found, explaining my thinking about the work each chunk was doing. Then I asked children to try this with another text, a text which I'd already boxed into sections.

Although we can anticipate lots of the difficulties that kids will encounter as we teach them, it is inevitable that new issues will emerge.

So, we keep our ears attuned, our eyes alert. We know from the start that as we teach a unit, we'll outgrow ourselves and our best teaching plans in leaps and bounds.

WRITE MINILESSONS

In writing workshops, kids generate ideas for writing, then they select one of those to develop. They make an overall plan on either a timeline, a story mountain or some boxes and bullets, and then they revise those plans. They try a few alternate leads—and then get started. They write with some tentativeness, expecting to revise what they write with input from others.

The process of authoring a unit of study is not so different. We generate ideas for a unit and then select one of these to develop. Then we make an overall plan for the unit and revise it. Eventually, we settle on a plan and get started. After all that planning and revising, we write the first word. Even then, we write knowing that our teaching plans will be what Gordon Wells refers to as "an improvable draft."

If teaching plans are only in our minds, or only coded into a few words in a tiny box of a lesson-plan book, then it's not easy to revise those plans. But ever since we human beings were cave dwellers, inscribing the stories of hunts on stony cave walls, we have learned that once we record our thoughts and plans, then the community can gather around those thoughts. Those thoughts can be questioned, altered, expanded. The ideas of one person can be added to the thoughts of another. In scores of schools where I work closely with teachers, we keep a binder for each unit of study. In that binder, we keep a collection of all the minilessons written that are related to each unit. Many of these are minilessons one teacher or another wrote, but others come from professional development teachers have attended or books they've read. In these binders, the teachers also deposit other supporting material.

Hints for Writing Minilessons:

1. **The Start of the Connection**

   Try to think of the first part of your Connection as a time to convey the reason for this minilesson. You are hoping to catch children's attention and to rally their investment. Fairly often, this is a time to step aside from writing for just a moment, telling a story or reliving a class event in a manner that will soon become a lead to (or metaphor for) whatever you will teach.

   If you have trouble writing the start of a minilesson, it is also possible to settle for simply saying, "Yesterday I taught you . . . ." and then referring to the exact words of yesterday's teaching point. These should usually be written on a chart, so gesture toward the chart as you talk. Ideally you can follow this with a memorable detail of someone who used yesterday's teaching point (a published author, you or a child). You can say something such as, "Remember that . . . ."

2. **The Teaching Point**

   This will only be a few sentences long but nevertheless it merits care and revision as it is the most important part of your minilesson. Plan to repeat the exact words of your teaching point at least twice in the minilesson. In order to learn to create teaching points, try temporarily staying within the template of these words or something very close to them. "Today, I will teach you that when writers . . . , we often find it helps to . . . We do this by . . . " The important thing to notice in this template is that we are not saying, "Today we will do this." A teaching point is not the assignment for the day! Instead, the teaching point is a strategy that writers use often in order to accomplish important writing goals. Then, too, notice that teaching points do not simply define the territory within which one will teach. That is, if a teaching point went like this: "Today I will teach you how to write good leads," then there would be nothing worth remembering in this teaching point!

3. **The Teaching**

   When planning how the teaching will go, begin by deciding what your method and materials will be. If you will be demonstrating using your own writing, go back and look at a few minilessons in which I used a similar method, and at first follow the template of these minilessons. You will probably see that I set children up to observe me by telling them what I hope they will notice and what they will do after I demonstrate. Then I tell the story of how I came to need the strategy. Then, I act out what one does first, next, and next in using this strategy. I often include in my demonstration an instance when I do something unhelpful, and then I correct myself, coming back on track. Throughout the demonstration, I tend to write only about four sentences; usually these are added to an ongoing piece that threads its way through much of the unit.

   I might demonstrate using a bit of a published author's text instead of my own writing, and again, if you decide to create a minilesson using that method, find instances when I did this and let them serve as an exemplar for you. You'll find that if I am demonstrating using a published author's text, I'll enact what the author probably did, prefacing my enactment with a phrase such as, "So and so probably did this. He probably . . . ."

   I might choose not to demonstrate. Instead, for example, I might talk about something and then show an example. These kinds of minilessons are more challenging to write, but again, I encourage you to find and follow a model as a way to induct yourself into this work.

4. **The Active Engagement**

   Almost always, this will be a time when children try the strategy that you have just taught, and they do so by writing-in-the-air (talking as if they are writing) to a partner. For example, if you have taught that toward the end of one's work on a text, a writer rereads her own writing to ask, "Does this make sense?" then you'll want to use the Active Engagement time as a chance to provide children with some scaffolded practice doing this. You have two common options. One option is for you to say, "So right now, while you sit in front of me, would you get out your own writing and read just the first paragraph as if you are a stranger, asking yourself, 'Does this make sense?' If you spot a place where it is confusing, put a question mark in the margin." The advantage of asking children to try the strategy this way is that you help children apply the minilesson to their own work and help them get started on their own work. The disadvantage is that sometimes kids can't use the teaching point of the day on just any paragraph (as they could in this example), and therefore it is not possible for them to find a place where the strategy applies and put the strategy into operation all within just a few short minutes. This portion of a minilesson shouldn't take more than four minutes! Then, too, you can't provide much scaffolding or do much teaching off this work because each child will be working with a different piece of writing.

You might, therefore, say, "Would you help me with my piece by becoming a reader of my next paragraph? Would Partner One read it quietly, aloud, and as you read, think, 'Does this make sense?' Partner Two, you listen and give your partner a thumbs up if yes, you think it is making sense." By using your writing for the Active Engagement, You'd have a common text to discuss if problems arise in applying the strategy. Also, when children have applied the strategy to your writing, they could also transfer the strategy to their own writing once the minilesson was over and they were on their own. Otherwise, the teaching of the minilesson won't carry into the workshop time, and may be less likely to carry into each child's writing life.

Sometimes the Active Engagement portion of the minilesson does not involve partner work; each child works individually, often guided by the teacher's nudges. Teachers listen in on what children do sometimes intervene to lift the level of a particular child's work. We often end the time by reporting back on the good work one child did.

5. **The Link**

During this portion of the minilesson, you will always repeat the teaching point verbatim, usually adding it to a chart as you do so. You won't have one amalgamated chart that lists every teaching point that has ever been taught! Each chart will feature a collection of strategies writers can use to accomplish a particular goal. That is, the title of the chart generally names the goal, and then below this there will be a growing list of strategies writers might draw upon to accomplish that goal. Charts lose their effectiveness if they are too long. Typically, charts do not contain more than five or six specific items.

Generally, the Link is a time for you to tell children when to use what you have taught them. You will be apt to say something like, "When you are (in this situation as a writer) and you want to (achieve this goal), then you might use any one of these strategies: (and you reread your charted list). Another option would be to use this strategy (and you add the new strategy to the list)." Usually, in the Link, you will say something like, "So today, you have lots of choices. You can do this, or that, or this, or that . . . ."

PLAN CONFERENCES, LETTERS TO PARENTS, RUBRICS, HOMEWORK . . . AND THE REST

Planning a unit can't be equated with just writing minilessons! First of all, once you have planned a sequence of minilessons, you can read through them imagining the challenges they will pose for your children. You'll be able to ascertain that for some minilessons, many of your children will need extra support, and those will be good places to plan small-group strategy lessons. You may decide that on some of those occasions, you will go from table to table, providing close-in demonstrations of whatever it is you hope children do first, then circling back for demonstrations of whatever you hope children do next. For these extra-challenging minilessons, you will probably want to plan follow-up minilessons, devising those after you study the particular ways in which your children are encountering difficulty.

Then, too, you'll want to plan how you will assess children's progress. You might think that the time to assess is at the end of a unit, but in fact, it is wise to mark mid-unit checkpoints. For example, in *Launching*, you can predict that after three or four days of collecting entries, you will want to check to see which of the children are writing about focused events, which are organizing their narratives chronologically, and which are storytelling rather than summarizing. In *Literary Essays*, you'll want to look over children's entries a few days into the study to see whether children have been gathering entries which contain possible thesis statements.

You can plan for any other aspect of your teaching as well. For example, you could plan how partnerships might be tweaked so that they support the goals of the unit. You might think about particular language lessons that English Language Learners may need in a unit. In *Personal Narrative*, for example, English Language Learners may need help writing in past tense and using temporal transition words. In *Breathing Life into Essays*, they may need support writing with logical transitions.

Because your units of study will be written down, you and your colleagues can put them on the table and think together about these plans. "What's good here that we can add onto?" you can ask. "What's not so good that we can fix?"

CHAPTER 10

SUPPORTING ENGLISH LANGUAGE LEARNERS

These units of study have been taught in thousands of New York City classrooms. The writing workshop's success across New York City has been dramatic and that success is especially poignant in schools filled with English Language Learners. It was no surprise to us to learn that since the writing workshop has been brought to scale across the city, results from the National Assessment for Educational Progress (NAEP) show that our ELLs have made especially dramatic progress.

Because the Teachers College Reading and Writing Project works primarily in New York City schools, where classrooms brim with English Language Learners, we spend a lot of time thinking about ways in which the writing workshop can be adjusted so that it is especially supportive for our ELLs.

It is clear that the writing workshop, specifically, and more generally, the structures of New York City's version of balanced literacy, are tailored to support English Language Learners. Language development is embedded in the structures of this version of balanced literacy. These classrooms are organized in such clear, predictable, consistent ways that children quickly become comfortable participating in their ongoing structures. Very early in the school year, ELL children come to understand that writing workshops start with the teacher giving a minilesson, and that during the minilesson they learn strategies that they are then expected to apply to their independent work. Children know that after the minilesson, they will be expected to write independently, and that the teacher will circulate around the room, conferring with individuals and with small groups. Children also know that they will be expected at some point to share their work with a partner (more on this later). When their writing time is over, children know that they need to put their materials away and gather in the meeting area (or with a partner) for a share. When teachers follow these routines day after day, students can focus their energy on trying to figure out how to do their work rather than on worrying over what they will be expected to do. The predictability of the workshop provides tremendous reassurance to a child who is just learning English, and this is amplified if workshop structures repeat themselves across other subject matters.

In addition, writing workshops are characterized by a consistent instructional language. The consistency of this language scaffolds each child's classroom experience, making it easier for a child who is just learning English to grasp the unique content that is being taught that day. For example, it helps that every minilesson starts in a predictable manner, with teachers saying, "Writers," and then reviewing the content of yesterday's minilesson, referencing a bullet on a chart. It helps children that every day the teacher encapsulates the day's lesson in a sentence or two(the teaching point) that is repeated often and written on a chart.

Of course, the predictability of the workshop also means that teachers needn't invent a new way each day to support English Language Learners. Because the same classroom structures are in place every day, solutions that help on Tuesday will also help on Wednesday, Thursday and Friday.

Then, too, the work that children do in the writing workshop always, inevitably, provides wonderful learning opportunities for English Language Learners. Because the child always chooses what she will write about, chooses the words she will use, chooses the people and places and themes that will be brought forth in the texts, chooses meanings that are vibrantly important to her, chooses the level of vocabulary and of sentence and text structures, and so forth, the writing workshop is *by definition* always individualized. Yet—and here is the really powerful thing—the writing workshop is also, by definition, utterly interpersonal. You try it. Write about the things that are on your mind. Put your mom on the page, or your son; capture that memory that haunts you. Now bring this page to the table when you gather with the people who live and work alongside you. Share the text. Talk about it. You will find that by sharing your writing, something happens that makes you and the

people with whom you shall see each other in a new way; sometimes it will almost seem as if you are seeing each other for the first time. You will see that if you share your writing with your colleagues, you will go through each school day with a different sense of yourself and of your workplace, and the same will be true for your ELLs. You'll understand that song, "No man is an island, no man stands alone. Each man's joy is joy to me, each man's grief is my own . . . ." For every one of us, the chance to work and learn in the presence of a community of others is invaluable. Could we possibly give anything more precious to our English Language Learners? To all our children?

But let us think now about specific ways in which each of the components of the writing workshop can be altered just a bit so that the workshop as a whole is especially supportive for ELLs. Of course, there is no such thing as "the" English Language Learner. Language learners, like all learners, differ one from the next in a host of ways. Two significant factors contributing to their unique needs will be the child's level of competence in his or her native language and the child's English proficiency.

TAILORING THE WRITING WORKSHOP TO SUPPORT CHILDREN IN ALL THE STAGES OF LEARNING ENGLISH

Support in the Preproduction and Early Production Stages of Learning English

It's critical that we, as teachers, think through how each of the components of a writing workshop can be altered to provide ELLs with the support they need. Second language learners go through predictable stages of language acquisition as they move to full fluency in English. When we plan the writing workshop, we need to think about how we are going to meet our children's needs as they develop English language skills and how we are going to adjust our expectations as children move toward full fluency.

Children who are in either the silent period (or preproduction stage) or in the early production stages of learning English will have few oral English skills but they will be listening carefully, trying to interpret what is going on around them. It is okay for children to be quiet at this stage, but we, as teachers, need to understand that they are taking in a lot of information. The English words, phrases and sentences which will make sense to them first will probably be the predictable sentences related to concrete classroom activities, such as, "Get your writing," and "Draw something on this paper," and "You can go to your seat now" or "Let's gather in the meeting area." Opportunities for listening, really listening, are important, and the expectation that these children will participate in the comings and goings of the class spotlights the importance of them learning the social language that is most within their grasp. It is definitely important that these children *are* being told, "Get out your pencil," and "Draw here," and "Let's gather in the meeting area," (with accompanying gestures) and that they are expected to do all these things along with the others.

The writing workshop is an especially rich context for language development because children are not only writing and listening; they are also talking—and much of that talk happens in the small, supportive structures of partnerships. Eventually, these partnerships will give children important opportunities to rehearse for writing, but when children are in the preproduction stage of learning English, a partnership with one other child could make the child at the early-production stage feel trapped, like a deer in the headlights, with nowhere to hide. Still, it is crucial that new arrivals are expected to join into the class as best they can from the start. There is never a time when new arrivals sit on the edge of the community, watching. Instead, the rug spot for the new arrival needs to be right in the center of the meeting area, and from the start, when children turn and

talk during the Active Engagement section of a minilesson, these children must know that they belong to a conversational group.

Children in the early stages of learning English benefit, however, from being in triads not partnerships; ideally one child in that triad will share the new arrival's native language but be more proficient in English, and the other will be a native speaker of English (and a language model).

Granted, children who are in the pre-production stage of learning English will mostly listen. Their more English-proficient partners can be shown how to speak with children who are at the beginning stages of learning English; like the teacher, more proficient partners can learn to use lots of gestures and to ask the child questions that can be answered with a yes or a no, a nod or a head shake.

I hope that I am making it clear that when a child in the first stages of acquiring English arrives in a classroom, the first goal is to make sure that child is immediately active and interactive. If this child is literate in his or her first language, than by all means, it is important for the child to write (and to read) in that language. If there are people in the classroom or the school who can speak the child's native language, we can rely on this buddy to convey to the child the kind of text that the class is writing, and some of the main ideas about that text. For example, this buddy might convey, "We are writing fiction stories, realistic ones with just a few characters in our stories and just a few different moments."

Whether or not the new arrival is literate in his first language, while that child writes as best he can in his first language, you will also want the child to begin doing some writing in English. Some teachers find that it helps for these children to have time-slots for first language and for English writing, with the child perhaps starting the writing workshop with fifteen minute to write in his language. (During this time, the child can write with volume that is comparable to other children and build his identity as a child who writes a lot.) But it is also important for this child to write in English.

Usually we start by asking the child who is at early stages of learning English to draw and label her drawing when writing in English. This, of course, is reminiscent of what we ask kindergarten and first-grade children to do. Of course, there is nothing "elementary" about learning a second language, and yet taking children new to English through the progression of work that younger children in a writing workshop experience has all sorts of advantages. After a child has drawn and labeled in English for a bit, we can ask the child to start writing in sentences. These children need the same range of paper choices that we normally offer to children in earlier grades. Examples can be printed from the CD-ROM available in the *Units of Study for Primary Writing* series. It is especially important that these children have access to paper that contains a large box on the top of a page, and several lines for writing under that box. The size of the box shrinks and number of lines increases as children develop proficiency in English. This progression of paper is an extremely powerful way to scaffold children's language development. Imagine that the child has written about a soccer game in her first language, and drawn a series of sketches showing what happened first, next, and last in the game. Then, with help from English-speaking children, the child labels each drawing with lots of English words, providing the child with a picture dictionary that is tailored to that child's exact story. It is not such a big step, then, to ask this child to use those words and write a sentence or two to accompany each of the child's drawings.

If a teacher has children who are in the early stages of English acquisition, it is especially important to provide them with extra help understanding the content of a minilesson. If there is an English as a Second Language teacher who is willing to provide support, this can also

be extremely beneficial. Some ESL teachers push in to classrooms, some ESL teachers pull out children for work in the ESL room. In either case, if classroom teachers and ESL teachers are provided with opportunities for planning together, the ESL teacher can support the children during writing workshop by preteaching the concepts and developing the vocabulary that will be necessary to understand what will be taught in the minilesson. For example, if the minilesson will teach children how to write with main ideas and support ideas, the ESL teacher might use a nonfiction content area book and lots of gestures to convey that the title of the book is the main idea or the big idea, and then to convey that some of the subtitles are support ideas (or smaller ideas). The teacher could reinforce the concept of ordination and subordination (without using those terms) by showing that the classroom represents a big topic, the library area could represent a subtopic.

There are ways to alter minilessons so as to support English language learners. First, we will want our minilessons to be as concise as possible. If you are working with such a population, you'll want to trim the minilessons in this series! Then, too, visuals can make a huge difference. It helps to draw and act as you talk. Sketch almost any story as you tell it. If you want to describe the way in which a writer can "stretch out" sections of a story, for example, it helps to tug on the ends of a rubber band whenever saying the term, "stretch out." We will also probably make a special point of using examples that children can relate to. It's helpful to repeat the teaching point more often with children who are just learning English.

Some teachers find that if we've used write-in-the-air to demonstrate something and want children to learn from our example, children profit from first retelling the teacher's version of the text before they then apply these principles to their own content. This leads some teachers to set up a double Active Engagement within many minilessons. Similarly, when we want children to turn and talk, it can help to set them up with cue cards. In *Breathing Life into Essays*, for example, we might give them cards that say "one example"..."another example...."

If the child has not received schooling in her first language or if that schooling has been especially interrupted, the child will face many more challenges. Expect this child to require extra support for a number of years. For children learning English, the writing workshop will provide a rich form of language education. Children will be learning to write, of course, but they will also learn to narrate, summarize, predict, describe, elaborate, question, to extend their vocabulary, and best of all, to use language to interact with each other and to set ideas and places, people and events onto the page.

Support in the Later Stages of Learning English

As children begin to acquire more fluency in English, they will be able to understand written and spoken English when they have concrete contexts (pictures, actions, sounds, and so on). As they develop these proficiencies, we often move them from triads to partnerships (or we nudge them to become one of the more vocal members of a triad, with a new preproduction ELL joining in as best he or she can). We know these learners will not always use correct syntax but we also know they can participate fully in partnership work.

As children become more proficient in English, their answers to questions will be more extended, but of course, their hold on English grammar and vocabulary will still be approximate. Again, partners (and teachers) can be coached to realize that this is not a time for correcting grammar. Instead, it is a time for extending what the child says. If the child points to a picture she has drawn as part of a story

she's written and says, "Mom," then we'll want to expand on this. "That's your mom?" [pause for nod] "You and your Mom" [pointing] "went in the car?" [pointing] "Where did you go?" [gesturing to illustrate that the question pertained to where the car drove]. If the child isn't sure how to answer, we can eventually supply options, "Did you go to the store? Or to the park?"

In order to help children bring a growing repertoire of language from the minilessons into their independent work, the teacher will often scaffold the writing that children do (and also the conversations that children have during work time with their partners) by providing them with conversational prompts. For example, in *Breathing Life into Essays*, the teacher might teach children to write or say, "I see...." and then to shift and write or say, "I think...." The thought can be elaborated on when the child learns to use transition phrases such as, "For example...." Children who are just learning English may rely heavily on these prompts, and teachers may even write cue cards for them.

It is important for teachers to celebrate the work that children at this stage of early emergent English are producing, focusing on the content and quality of the story not on the correctness of the syntax. These children are taking risks and teachers need to help them to feel successful.

But meanwhile, children also need instruction. For example, if children are writing personal narratives, a teacher might teach and then post transition words that show that a little time has passed such as, "Then...," "Later...," "After a while...," "Five minutes later...," or "Next...." The teacher might remind children that in their stories, as they move from one dot on a timeline to the next, they will often use a time word to show that time has passed. To practice this, the teacher might ask one partner to tell another what he or she did since walking in the classroom, remembering to insert words that show the passage of time. When partners meet, teachers can suggest that they talk through the sequence of events on each child's timeline, using time words as the storyteller progresses from one dot on the timeline to the next. Each child will also benefit from having a list of these transition words during work time, itself.

Support in Learning Academic English

As important as it is for us, as teachers, to tailor work time during the writing workshop so that children in the early stages of English acquisition receive the help they need, it is equally important for us to be cognizant that children who are in later stages of language acquisition also need special support. When children reach intermediate fluency, they demonstrate increased levels of accuracy and are able to express their thoughts and feelings in English. They often sound as if their English is stronger than it is—this is because although these children have developed conversational skills, often they still do not have academic English language skills. These children often seem to be very proficient in English. They have a strong command of social English, and can use English to chat with each other, to learn what the teacher expects them to do, to talk about the events of the day. They may sound "fluent" in social conversation where complex structures can be avoided, but it is often difficult to follow them when they describe events from another time and place.

The challenge for these children is that they need now to learn academic English; in order to learn this, they need input from people who can provide strong language models and from skilled teachers. At this stage it is very important for teachers to work on elaboration and specificity so as to help children use more descriptive and extended language. It is also important for these children to be partnered with children for whom English is their first language, children who can function as strong language models. The interesting thing is that often, when teachers have a handful of children who are in the earliest stages of language acquisition and a handful who are further along, teachers devote most of their special attention to the children who are the newest to English. However, the truth is that if we set new arrivals up with the proper invitations to work, support-structures from other children, and ways of being interactive, they can learn a huge amount from each other. Meanwhile, children who have a good command of social English but not of academic English need help which is less readily available from the peer group.

One way to determine whether a child needs help with academic English is to talk to the child about the story in a novel or about something that happened in another time and place. Invite the child to retell an episode from the book or from the child's experience; listen well. If the child's language is such that you have a hard time really piecing together what she is intending to communicate, chances are good this child needs support with "academic English." That is, the phrase 'academic' English does not refer only to the language that is used in discipline-based studies. The phrase refers to the language that a person must use in order to communicate about a time and place which are distant and unfamiliar, which must be created by the words.

Children who need help with academic English will profit from explicit instruction tailored to their needs. For example, these children benefit from instruction in connectives. They tend to write in simple sentences, linked together with the connector, *and*. It is important for children to study connectors because when English language learners learn to read as well as to write, these can become a source of confusion. Many readers assume that sentences are arranged in chronological order. However, in many sentences, that assumption is incorrect, for example, "I went to the office because the principal called for me over the PA system." In small-group instruction, then, teachers will want to provide English Language Learners with explicit instruction to help them understand connectors, tenses, pronoun references, and so forth.

Of course, English Language Learners also need support in developing a rich vocabulary, and again, children benefit from explicit instruction. If a child overuses a word such as *nice* or *beautiful*, a teacher will want to help children learn that there are many different, more precise words the child could use. Is the person lovely? Impressive? Unusual? Dignified? Cute? Some teachers help children to develop word files, with the overused word at the center of a card, and five variations of that word around the edges. Children keep these cards on hand throughout the day and look for opportunities to use specific words orally (some teachers ask children to place a check mark beside a word each time they use it orally).

This word bank would also be on hand when the child writes. If a child decides that her beloved mother is not dignified but cute, then the child's personal connection to the word will make it more memorable than had the child merely encountered it in a class on vocabulary.

Children learning English will need support as they come to understand and to use figurative language. Of course, literature is filled with metaphor and simile, as are the minilessons in these series. Children who are just on the brink of learning academic English will profit from some small-group instruction which gives them access to literary devices.

Similarly, if children are writing about a particular subject, the teacher or an English-speaking buddy may want to help the child build a domain-specific vocabulary to draw upon as he or she writes. If the child is writing about attending a carnival, the child would benefit from having a conversation about his experience at the carnival. This sort of rehearsal is important to every writer, but it can provide an extra language support to the English Language Learner who is ready to learn precise vocabulary.

OUR TEACHING IN EVERY UNIT CAN SUPPORT WRITING GOALS—AND LANGUAGE GOALS

When teachers approach a unit of study we need to think about the language needs of ELL children in the classroom: What are the language skills that our children need to have in order to understand the work that they are being asked to do? We need to think not only about the writing skills and strategies that will be developed in a unit, but also about the language language skills the unit will support. We need to think about the vocabulary, the idiomatic expressions, the connectives, the conjunctions, and about the grammar we want children to develop in a unit. There has to be a plan for content and a plan for language, side by side.

When approaching a unit in essay writing, for example, we can anticipate that we'll be teaching children to explain, describe, compare, categorize and question. We can anticipate that mostly we'll be helping children write in present tense, and that they'll benefit from learning connectives such as *if*, *when*, *because*, *for example*, *another example*, and so forth. We can plan that we might provide scaffolds such as a chart of phrases and we can know in advance that children may need help with instructional terms such as *fact*, *example*, *reason*, *thought*, and *idea*. We know we may teach the language of comparison, including, for example, the use of the '-er' and '-est' word endings, as in 'big, bigger, biggest.'

The power of written curriculum is that a group of teachers can hold our hopes for teaching in our hands, and talk and think together about how we can take our own best ideas and make them better. One of the most important ways to make our teaching stronger is to think, "How can we give all children access to this teaching?" The wonderful thing about a workshop is that it is incredibly supportive for English Language Learners—but if you bring your best idea to the table, you can make the writing workshop even more supportive.

Preparing for Standardized Writing Tests

As I write this chapter, my son Evan is downstairs, working with a stopwatch at his side, practicing yet one more time for the writing component of his April SAT exam. He and I know that on that exam, he will have twenty-five minutes to read a prompt, then to plan, write, and edit a well-constructed essay. In the essay, he's been told to reference a classic novel and an episode from history. He also needs to write with an opening hook, an introductory anecdote, a thesis statement which lays out a framing idea, and two body paragraphs, each beginning with a transition and ending with references to his thesis statement and his framing idea. The essay will ideally end with yet another anecdote, with a nod to the thesis, and with a new twist on the original idea. And Evan needs to do all this in twenty-five minutes! Frankly, despite all the advantages that Evan has been given, he and I are both sweating over the demands of this high-stakes test.

Meanwhile, he will no sooner finish the SAT exam than it will be time for the ACT exam, followed by a whole series of AP exams. And of course, Evan is not alone. Children in all our schools are being subjected to high-stakes assessments as never before, and some of these assessments have life-changing consequences for children. There was a time when fourth and eighth grades were "the testing grades." Now tests tyrannize every grade, every year.

That tyranny is felt by teachers as well as by students. Our students' performances on standardized assessments have very real consequences on our right to teach according to our best beliefs. It is an understatement, then, to say that standardized tests have important implications for those of us who teach children. It is therefore important to take into account the demands of high-stakes writing assessments when we plan a yearlong curriculum in the teaching of writing.

KNOWLEDGE IS POWER

Knowledge of standardized tests can allow you to avoid being victimized by the testing and test-prep industry, and to teach test prep with the same clarity with which you teach anything else.

Several years ago, Kate Montgomery (the editor of this series), Donna Santman and I coauthored a book about standardized reading tests entitled, *A Teacher's Guide to Standardized Reading Tests: Knowledge Is Power*. When doing the research for that book, my colleagues and I came to realize that many of us were painfully uninformed about the reading assessments that hold such sway over us and our children. The fact that so many teachers are not knowledgeable about the tests is not surprising. Teachers often regard the tests with hostility—we don't want to give them any more attention than is absolutely required! But a lack of knowledge about the tests will backfire, making us easy victims. This remarkably unprincipled industry feeds on developing test-anxiety in teachers and school leaders and then providing test prep materials, at a price, to supposedly allay those anxieties. Our study further convinced us that much of what was being taught in the name of test prep added to students' confusion, consolidated their unhelpful test-taking habits, and in general, wreaked havoc. It was fascinating and frightening for us to find that teachers who would never dream of importing random bits of curriculum into their school day, who would never consider shoving any old materials that crossed their desks at their kids, were doing this with the test-prep materials. Meanwhile, those test-prep materials came at us from all sides, presumably from administrators whose anxieties translated into similar practices. It was as if everyone, at every level, was so anxious and out of his element that instead of constructing a crystal-clear approach to teaching test prep, we disregarded everything we knew about curriculum and teaching in the name of preparing kids for the craziness of standardized reading tests.

Thankfully, writing assessment has not yet escalated into quite the same frenzy. My clear suggestion is this: don't let a fear of writing assessment derail you from teaching writing well! Teach writing rigorously, following the pathways laid out in this series, and I promise you that the results will be dramatic, palpable, obvious, and lasting. I have received not dozens but hundreds—perhaps thousands—of responses to the primary series of books, with teachers saying, "I would never have believed that my kids could do so much." Those kids will be growing up and coming into your upper-elementary classrooms, so right there, you'll find that the tests are less daunting. And if you teach writing well and do so within a curriculum that emphasizes the structures of narrative and essay writing, your kids will be absolutely ready for you to show them how to take all they know and use it to shine on those assessments.

Writing assessments for children in the elementary grades differ, state by state. Some assessments require students to produce a narrative, others ask for one version or another of an essay (this is sometimes a literary essay, sometimes a personal/persuasive essay, and sometimes a persuasive letter shaped like an essay). Some writing assessments do not channel children toward one kind of writing or another, leaving this open. The units of study in these books will go a very long way toward preparing your students for any one of these assignments, but it will be important for you to analyze the demands put on your children so that you can tweak these units, if this seems called for, and provide the supplemental instruction your children need.

Of course, the first thing you will think about is that on their assessments, your children will need to read and analyze a prompt or an assignment so that they understand what they are being called to do and can go about planning a piece of writing which meets requirements set forth by someone else. As part of this, they need to be able to read their own writing with objective eyes, seeing ways in which it does and does not meet the criterion for success, and also seeing ways in which the paper could be altered so it would be judged more successful. These two skills are closely related, and together translate into the fact that students need to be able to read and analyze an assignment or prompt, to create a mental representation of what it is they are expected to do, and to proceed, letting their work fit the contours of what someone else expects them to do.

Then, too, in every state, children will be asked to write quickly, on demand, and in a relatively correct and well-organized fashion from the start; again, this will be addressed in some detail later in this chapter.

Although kids will not, in the writing workshop, be accustomed to writing under a stopwatch in response to a prompt or an assignment, the writing that they will be expected to produce on their assessments will be simpler versions of what they have been writing all along. That is, if a fourth grader is asked to write a narrative on a state test, the narrative the child produces will be vastly more impressive if she even gestures toward writing with detail, making characters talk, bringing out the internal as well as the external story, developing the heart of the story and so forth as she has learned to do in this yearlong curriculum. This curriculum expects much more of nine-, ten- and eleven-year-olds than any state test! Similarly, if children are asked to write an essay (or to persuade or argue), the child's writing will be vastly more impressive if the child remembers to develop a thesis with supportive claims, to embed stories which make the point, to return back to the thesis statement often. All of this WILL be asked of children when they are sixteen years old and hoping to ace the SAT exam, but there won't be any state which asks or expects nine-year-old children to do this.

On the other hand, there may be some small ways in which your state's assessments require something more than what children have learned through the units of study. For example, when children are asked to respond to quotations, they will need to reference texts and, in some instances, to ascertain and acknowledge the point of view (or bias) of a particular text. Similarly, by the time children are in middle school, some states expect that a persuasive (expository) essay will include a section in which the writer acknowledges and refutes opposing arguments. You will want to review your state assessments to determine

if there are any ways in which they ask children to do something a bit more than what they will learn through this yearlong curriculum.

And yes, there will be some things you need to teach under the auspices of test prep. When you do this teaching, remember that you will want to use the same methods to teach test prep that you use to teach anything else. Curriculum writers from the test prep company Stanley-Kaplan recently attended several Teachers College Reading and Writing Project institutes and then met with me to ask for my blessing in hiring a Project staff developer as a consultant to them as they wrote a series of test prep minilessons books. They did write those books—a whole series of them, each patterned after these *Units of Study* books, each containing minilessons which begin with a connection that includes a teaching point, and each of which follows this architecture of minilessons. My point is not to endorse those materials, my point is that if Kaplan, which has a tremendous knowledge of standardized tests and yet has hardly been a bastion of progressive teaching methods, has decided that writing workshop teachers could use workshop methods to teach a brief test-prep unit, then surely you and I should feel confident if we come to this same conclusion!

TESTS THAT CALL FOR PERSUASIVE OR EXPOSITORY WRITING

What do children need to know and be able to do in order to perform well on assessments that ask for persuasive or expository writing? How do these expectations align with and diverge from the writing skills developed in these *Units of Study*?

The first job is not for *students* to analyze prompts and internalize criterion, it is for *you and I* to do this. We need to do this while also keeping in mind what children will and will not have already learned to do. That way, we can plan ways to teach children how to apply what they know to the assessment and we can design teaching to help them learn what they may not yet know. Prompts which ask children to argue, persuade, or take a position and give reasons are common and I suspect these will become increasingly common as SAT-style tests trickle down into lower and lower grades.

Let's pause for just a moment to think about the SAT exams—that is, about the writing requirement that children will need to respond to six, seven or eight years *after* they are with us (and that is a long time).

On the SAT exam, students are given an assignment such as this: "Do you believe that that which doesn't kill you makes you stronger? Write an essay supporting your point of view. Use texts, experiences and observations to support your position."

The initial question can change: What is your opinion of the claim that honesty is not the best policy? What is your opinion of the claim that without knowledge of the past, we cannot truly understand the present? Of the claim that sometimes making a bad decision is better than making no decision at all? That disagreement leads to progress? That censorship is sometimes merited? In all of these instances, students are asked to write in a fashion that very closely resembles the essays they are taught to write in these *Units of Study*.

Granted, students who are writing their SAT exam essays are told to begin their essays with a hook, which might be a rhetorical question or a personal anecdote. For example, Evan began his essay on facing difficulties with a ministory about caving with his peers, crawling headfirst into a tunnel-like cave, then feeling a lump of fear and deciding to persevere, realizing that facing difficulties can make you stronger. In *Breathing Life into Essays* we downplayed the importance of a catchy lead. But teachers could make the decision to spotlight this facet of essay writing.

Then, in their SAT essays, students need to turn the question into a thesis, a claim. Evan's (very expensive) SAT

tutors have assured him that it is totally acceptable to write something strictly based on the prompt such as, "I believe that what doesn't kill us can make us stronger." Then writers must include what the makers of SAT exams refer to as a "framing idea." Your children will think of it as one, overarching reason for the thesis statement: "I believe that what doesn't kill us can make us stronger *because we learn to push past our limitations.*" Then, on SAT essays, students are expected to write two body paragraphs and in each, they are expected to refer to and then talk about one example that supports this claim. Ideally, in one paragraph, the student will refer to an example from either literature or history; in the other paragraph, the writer could again do that or could draw on personal experience. Each body paragraph needs a topic sentence that begins with a transitional word or phrase and then also refers back to the thesis or framing idea. One body paragraph might begin, "Just as I faced fears when crawling into that cave, so, too, Hamlet, the protagonist of Shakespeare's tragedy, needed to face his limitations." The next body paragraph would also stack evidence, building on the previous example, with a topic sentence that might start, "The need to face difficulties is evident not only in literature but also in history." Finally, in the ending paragraph, the writer must restate the thesis statement, and refer back to the examples. The essay will have even more flair if the writer can add a little twist to the end. My son is practicing finding a way to bring the phrase, "in order to make a better world," into the last sentence of almost every trial-run essay he's written!

My point in detailing this is simply this: as you read this, those of you who have studied the *Units of Study* in personal and literary essay will see that the *Units of Study* teach third graders to do most of what eleventh graders are required to do! So, you can rest assured that yes, indeed, these *Units of Study* will provide your children with the preparation they need.

Remember, during this section I am specifically addressing the times when elementary students are asked to write persuasive or expository essays. These prompts are different than prompts that ask students simply to *address a topic*—to tell about an experience you remember—without specifying how students are to approach that topic. In those cases, the writer will need to define the kind of writing for himself. Prompts that call for expository or persuasive writing are also different from those that ask students to write narratives: "Write about one time in your life that you remember well."

For now, let me say that if our intermediate students are asked to write expository or persuasive pieces, these will be significantly lighter versions of the SAT prompts I've detailed. Students may be asked: "Do you think students should wear uniforms to school? Tell why or why not, and give reasons." This prompt could have a different spin, starting with the same question about school uniforms (or whether standardized tests are wise, or whether recess is important) but the invitation to argue for one's point of view is followed with an attempt to make the exam feel more "real-life." For example, students may be asked: "Write a letter to the school principal arguing your point of view. Be sure to give reasons to support your opinion." Sometimes the test asks elementary students to address claims such as these: "Decisions (mistakes, challenges, classes, people) can change lives. Tell about a decision (or a mistake, a challenge, a class, a person) that/who taught you an important lesson."

Sometimes students will be asked to write persuasive or expository pieces in response to a text they have read: "In such and such text, what does the main character learn about friendship? Support your answers with details from the text." Or "In such and such text, do you think so and so was a good friend? Explain why or why not. Use examples from the text."

Sometimes children are asked to argue a point, and to do so by providing reasons that will be available to them in the texts they are asked to read. For example, after reading two articles about the harm that pollution is causing birds, children may be asked to write in response to this question: "Do you think pollution is endangering birds? Give reasons to support your answer and use examples from both texts to support your argument."

It is important for us to read a prompt or an assignment and see the kind of text that students are being asked to write. When I analyze most of these assignments, it seems to me that the most demanding ones ask us to teach students to do these things:

- *Our students need to be able to write a crystal clear thesis in which they make a claim, rather than stating a fact or asking a question.* This claim is generally related to the prompt, but if the prompt asks "Do you think children should spend holidays with their family?" or "Do you think this character was a good friend?" the student needs to not only state his or her point of view on the question, but also provide a reason, probably using the connector *because*. For example, the student might write, "I think children should spend holidays with their families because it makes families closer," or "Charlotte, the main character in *Charlotte's Web*, is a good friend to Wilbur because she does everything she can to save him from being killed."

- *Our students need to provide more than one example to support the thesis and each must be linked to the thesis.* Children need to learn to preface examples with a transitional word, phrase, or sentence. This transition before each example might be a topic sentence that sets up the support paragraph, one topic sentence for each example and for each paragraph. In fact, however, it is very rare for children in third through fifth grade to be expected to support their thesis across several paragraphs. However, if children are doing this in school anyhow and if enough time is provided, you might suggest children do write two support paragraphs when writing their on-demand essay—paragraphing reminds a writer (and the assessor) to pay attention to structure. The bare-bones expectation for persuasive or expository writing, however, is simply that the child makes a claim—"I think children should spend time with their families because this makes families closer"—and then elaborates with an example or two, each prefaced with a transitional phrase. It might read, "One example is that last summer I went camping with my family...." And, later, "Another example occurred last week when..." Or, better yet, the transitions could be stacked, "I learned that spending vacations with my family made us closer *not only* when we went camping together, *but also* when we...."

- *Children ideally learn to unpack their examples after they've laid them out.* This tends to make essays very strong, though it is usually not required. Unpacking the example involves returning to the claim, and explicitly talking about how the example illustrates the claim. "This story about when I went camping with my family shows that families become closer when vacationing together. My family is usually too busy to spend time together but when we went camping, we became closer by...."

- *Our students need to learn to write a concluding sentence or two in which they restate their initial claim and refer to their examples.* Ideally the writer adds a little twist to this section of the essay, perhaps by referring to a greater good, or to a larger lesson, such as "When you sit down to think up all the fun things that you can do on your next vacation, be sure to consider spending time with your family."

I describe teaching to these ends in great depth during the units of study on personal and literary essays. Once a teacher has studied the assessments, then, and related them to the *Units of Study,* it will be important to reassure students and their parents that when test day arrives, children will simply be asked to write a kind of thing they have been writing all along in the writing workshop. You will want to talk with students about how you will get them ready for the odd context that comes with testing situations—this writing is timed and written in response to a prompt.

It is important for us to look over the task and find a way to say to our students, "You definitely know how to do this already! This will be no big deal for you at all!" If that is not the case—if there ARE writing muscles students need to succeed on your district's assessment, then by all means weave these into your own version of the *Units of Study* in writing or into curriculum in other subjects. No matter what, you will need to approach test prep having already taught students the skills they will need to draw upon, so that test prep is simply a matter of showing children how easy it is to draw on the muscles they've developed elsewhere to produce something within the new (and yes, stressful) context.

TESTS THAT CALL FOR NARRATIVE WRITING

What do children need to know and be able to do in order to perform well on assessments that ask for narrative writing? How do these expectations align with and diverge from the writing skills developed in these *Units of Study*?

Some assessments will ask children to write narratives rather than to make and defend claims. The prompt might direct children to "Write a story about a time when you overcame a challenge (learned something new, made something special, met someone who changed you, were given a present, opened a door and found something surprising...). Include a beginning, a middle and an end, and write with details." Sometimes, instead, children will be asked to create short fiction. For example, they may be asked to write a story about a picture of a little girl and a dog standing under an umbrella, with rain pouring down around them. Perhaps there is something else in the scene—say, a kitten who is drenched, or a taxi cab approaching.

When children are asked to write a story, they will be expected to do exactly what they have learned in the *Units of Study*. That is, they will need to decide *who* is doing *what* in this story, and to imagine a timeline of events. If the writer writes all about the girl under the umbrella— "There is a girl under the umbrella. She is dry because of the umbrella. She is wearing a dress...."— then the writer would not fare well on this assessment. The task is to tell a story. The child would fare far better if he instead relied on what he'd learned in *Launching the Writing Workshop* and *Improving the Quality of Narrative Writing* and began the story with the main character doing or saying something, "'Move in close to me,' Hannah said to Rufus, her German shepard. 'This umbrella is big enough for both of us.' Just then, ..."

When children are asked to write narratives, the most important thing is that they do just that—write a Small Moment. Their stories will receive better ratings if they include:

- dialogue

- a character feeling something strong and therefore trying to do something

- details, especially descriptive details of the setting

- a resolution or a character learning a lesson

This last element of resolution can be created by the writer standing back from the story and writing a sentence or two of "reflection" on it: "That was the day when he learned..." or, "Now, years later, she still remembers that time because...."

FROM WRITING WORKSHOP TO WRITING-TO-THE-PROMPT

It is late March as I write this chapter, and my son has agreed to spend half an hour on many days of his spring vacation, practicing writing-to-a-prompt, with a cell phone (masquerading as a stop watch) beside him. His SAT exam is two weeks away, and now is a good time for Evan to prep for that exam. When kids are subjected to high-stakes tests, there is no question that we need to set them up for success on those tests, and one part of this will entail teaching children how to read, analyze, and respond to prompts and other forms of writing assignments. But let me be clear: Evan is spending *two weeks* before the SAT exam practicing writing-to-the-prompts. This writing-to-the-prompt is a wonderful form of test prep, but it would be a lousy writing curriculum. He is able to rally what it takes to write-to-the-prompt because of the rich writing life which his teachers have given him all along.

I sometimes encounter schools where concern for test scores has led teachers to substitute a daily drill of test prep for writing instruction. Thankfully, I do not find it necessary to spend a great deal of time arguing that a steady diet of writing-to-the-prompt couldn't possibly take the place of a rigorous writing curriculum because the student work speaks for itself. I simply display our kids' work and say "Do your kids write like this? Like this?" Children's work speaks for itself, and it is inevitably the case that children who are taught to write well have vastly more resources to draw upon when they are asked to write under timed conditions in response to an assigned prompt.

But of course, it is still important to teach children to read and analyze the prompt. In the schools I know best, teachers ask children to read the prompts very carefully, and to look especially for the kind of writing they are asked to produce. Teachers sometimes ask children to circle the verb that tells what sort of writing they are to do. Does the prompt ask for them to argue? Convince? Tell a story? Explain? Those words will give writers a clue about what is expected, but they will also want to look for and underline words that name the genre they are writing. Are they being asked to write an essay? A story? A letter to convince?

The most important mental work that a child must do when analyzing a prompt is determining what the test calls for, and then fitting this call to action into his knowledge of how to write well. That is, if the child reads the prompt and learns that he is to write about a day when he felt scared, he needs to decide whether he will write this as a story, calling to mind all he knows about writing focused narratives, or as an essay, calling to mind all he knows about writing according to what he will think of as a "boxes-and-bullets" structure.

Of course, responding to prompts is immeasurably easier if children have writing experience to draw upon! Imagine what it must be like for a child who is asked to write a story about the picture of a girl, holding an umbrella, if that child does not know what writers do to go about writing a story. Imagine what it must be like for a child to be asked to argue that pollution is harming birds, drawing on information in two articles, if that child isn't accustomed to writing a concise, clear claim and supporting that claim with reasons and examples!

Test prep is no big deal, when writers enter into it having already developed the muscles they need to draw upon. But test prep alone can't possibly prepare our kids for the hurdles they will be expected to get over. For that, they need to be actively engaged in the writing process, thoroughly and often.

CHAPTER 12

ASSESSMENT

Our student writers put marks on the page and we, as teachers of writing, read the writing but also read the writer. We read as a reader, responding to the heartache and adventure, humor and information, that each child has encoded onto the page, laughing and gasping and inquiring in response to what we find there. We also read as a teacher of writing, noticing what the child has tried to do, has done, and can almost do.

Assessment occurs in little and big ways throughout every minute of the teaching my colleagues and I have described. As a school year unfurls, not only our curriculum but also our assessments change.

ASSESSMENT THAT INFORMS US AS WE DEVELOP A CURRICULAR CALENDAR

Toward the end of a school year or the start of the summer, when teachers across a grade level—or a lone teacher, if need be—devote a good deal of time to planning the upcoming year's curriculum, it is crucial to begin by assessing the year that is ending and the work our departing students have done during that year. We want to reflect on our teaching, on the work our students have done, and on the progress our students have (and have not) made. We do all this with an eye toward growing new curricular plans for the year ahead.

- What worked? Did my teaching feel especially vital and strong during particular units of study? What made it work then? How can I build on this so that more of my teaching feels this way in the year ahead?

- What didn't work? Where did my teaching seem to flounder? What lessons can be drawn from that? How can I make curricular (and other) plans for the year ahead so that my teaching gets stronger? Should I tackle different units of study? Secure more support for particular units of study? Develop my own muscles for teaching particular things? What game plan could I develop that might help me outgrow myself?

- What have students learned? In looking over my students' written products, what have almost all of my students learned to do as a result of my teaching? How can I be sure to provide next year's students with these same opportunities—and help next year's students go even farther?

- What do students need to learn? In what ways could my students' work be dramatically strengthened? Obviously, it will take more than curricular plans to strengthen student work, but how can I design units of study that will help take students on the journey I have in mind for them?

ASSESSMENT THAT INFORMS US AS WE PLAN FOR THE FIRST DAYS OF SCHOOL

Summer has a way of slipping away quickly, and all of a sudden a new academic year is upon us, with a host of new children. It is crucial for us to make real contact with each and every child as quickly as we possibly can. Children need to come into our classroom and feel seen and heard. They need this instantly—all of them. How helpful it is if we give ourselves a head start!

Toward the end of each academic year, many schools organize what some people call "up and down" visits. The fifth-grade teachers spend a week (or a day) teaching fourth grade, the fourth-grade teachers teach third grade, and the third-grade teachers, second grade. Ideally, these visits happen with the host teacher in the classroom, but usually isn't possible. The visiting teacher then follows the host teacher's plans (the host teacher may meanwhile be at his or her feeder-grade level). In either case the visiting teacher learns something about the nature and abilities of the children he or she will be teaching next year. The following September, the teachers can deliberately create consistency across the two years by reminding children what they were able to do at the end of the preceding year and telling them this will be the starting point for the new year. This makes a world of difference; too often teachers' expectations do not move children along a thoughtful gradient of difficulty from year to year. For example, children may be writing two six-page books a week at the end of second grade, then move on to third grade teachers who act pleased if they produce half a page in a day's writing workshop!

Some teachers find it helps to write children's parents a letter in the summer. "I know my teaching will be strongest if I connect with your child as quickly as I can. Could you take a few minutes to write and tell me about your daughter? Tell me about her passions and her worries; tell me about her friendships and her family. What does she like to do when she has a free day?" When we know our children as individuals, it is much easier to teach them.

Assessment must occur continually as we teach writing. The child does something—anything—and we, as teachers, think, "What is this child showing me? What might the child be trying to do? Able to do? What seems to be just beyond the child's independent grasp?" The child acts, and the teacher interprets those actions and thinks, "How can I best respond?"

The challenge in writing about assessment is that assessment happens in so many ways, for so many purposes, that it is hard to pin down. Assessment is the thinking teacher's mind work. It is the intelligence that guides our every moment as a teacher.

GUIDING PRINCIPLES FOR ASSESSMENT

When we, as teachers, assess a child as a writer, we try to discern what the child can do independently so that we can determine the next step this child should take. Just as readers benefit if teachers help them progress along a gradient of difficulty, help them read books that are just a tiny bit beyond their independent reach, so too writers need instruction that scaffolds them to extend what they can do one notch farther. The curriculum laid out in these *Units of Study* suggests one trail along which writers develop, but there are lots of lines of growth for writers, and a skilled teacher can note what a child is doing and where she could, with help, be able to go along any one of those lines of growth.

For example, the teacher can look at a child's ability to organize non-narrative writing. Can the child distinguish topic-based subcategories so that information on "feeding my dog" is in a different place that information on "training my dog"? If the child can do this, can she or he also organize the information within any subcategory according to some principle? Is there some logic—any logic—informing the sequence of information in the "feeding my dog" section?

Teachers of writing need to be able to look at a piece of writing with a particular growth line in mind, name what the child can do along that growth line, and imagine what a logical next step might be. This assessment is necessary in order to provide children with the scaffolds they need to develop as writers. What a child can do at one moment with support, he or she should be able to do at another moment with independence.

Our assessments will be more sound if, at any one time, we deliberately choose the lens through which we look. If we don't consciously make this choice, we probably apply different criteria to different children. That is, without even realizing we are doing so, we may end up looking at the strong writers' work with an eye toward organization and looking at less experienced writers' work only for spelling and penmanship. Of course, there are countless possible lenses through which teachers could view their students as writers. How are children doing at storytelling rather than summarizing a narrative? At elaborating in ways that build significance? At spelling sight words correctly? At writing story endings? At producing a lot of work? At getting started writing without needing a personal nudge? At rereading their own work? At writing with detail?

It is sometimes worthwhile to look over the entire class, thinking, "How are all my children doing in any one area?" For example, we could ask, "How are all my children doing at writing stories in which a character moves sequentially through time?" This will probably result in our gathering clusters of children together and providing each cluster with some small-group strategy lessons. We may, at times, decide to look across all our children in order to assess a particular aspect of their work. We could look at something as simple as the amount of text a child is producing in a given writing workshop. Which children wrote at least a page-and-a-half today? Which wrote approximately a page? Which wrote half a page or less? We could, on the other hand, look at something less obvious. For example, we could look at the conjunctions children use in their sentences, which will tend to reveal their sentence complexity. We could look at the scale of their revision work. How many add and delete pages? Paragraphs? Phrases only?

Of course, the reason to group children is so that we are ready to differentiate instruction in the area of consideration. The discovery that some children are revising by altering phrases only is not an assessment of them so much as of us—and it is a wake-up call as well. Obviously, there is nothing in the child's genetic makeup that means the child only revises minute portions of his or her text! How will we teach those children so that this changes?

If assessments are going to inform instruction, it is crucial that we understand that the questions are always "What can a child do now?" and "What can a child almost do now?" The question "What can't a child do?" doesn't tend to inform instruction, because there will always be vast terrain that is beyond any given learner. Just because a child can't synthesize information from six sources or write citations with correct footnotes does not mean this is what we should teach him to do these things! But if we notice that a child makes characters in her drawings speak in speech balloons but has never yet made characters in her written stories speak, then it is logical to think we could perhaps show her how to bring the contents of those speech balloons into the text of her story. The job of assessment, then, involves finding the growing tip of a child's writing development and nurturing it.

When we are learning a skill, it's great fun to see ourselves getting better. Whether we are learning to play softball or swim or roller-skate, it helps to have concrete goals and to be able to see and record our progress toward those goals. The fledgling swimmer works hard to swim from one side of the pool to the other. When he meets this goal, he is ready for the next one and will work hard to achieve it.

Writing development occurs on lots of fronts, and children can't consciously tackle all the goals we have in mind. They need to have a palpable, concrete sense of what good work entails and to be able to chart their progress toward at least some fairly obvious aspects of achieving it. Therefore, it is important to show children examples of good work that are within their reach and supply them with guidelines they can apply when assessing their own work.

It is also important that children join with us in noticing the pathway they've already traveled and in setting goals for the next phase of their development. People learn as much or more from attention to growth and celebrations of progress as from critique. Taking this into account, frank discussion should occur often in

a conference. "I see you are able to do this now and that is great—what I think you need to reach toward now is this. Let me help you get started doing that, with me nearby to help. Okay, now see if you can keep going without me. Wow! You did it! From now on, do this whenever you write."

Whenever we assess what children know and can do as writers, it is important that we understand that the children are reflections of the effectiveness of our work with them. Whether we are classroom teachers, building principals, or involved staff developers, we need to understand that the information about what our children can and cannot do as writers is also information about what we have and have not done in our respective roles. What have we done well? What must we begin to do better? What could be the sources of trouble? How might we best respond? The most valuable assessment is always self-assessment.

OPPORTUNITIES FOR ASSESSMENT

Writers' Notebooks

The good news about teaching writing is that children regularly give us demonstrations of what they know and can do. The first step toward becoming a teacher who assesses children's writing is being sure that each child has a writer's notebook and a folder containing his or her current work. Each writer should also have a different portfolio containing samples of work accumulated throughout the year or throughout several years.

The most important work to save is that produced by the child's own hand. That is, there are lots of reasons to edit, word-process, and publish children's writing, but for the purpose of assessment, the writing that really needs to be dated, organized, saved, and studied are the rough drafts of what children themselves have written.

The first tool for assessment, then, is the writer's notebook. Page through any child's notebook and one is immediately given a window onto this child as a writer. What are the range of topics that the child tends to write about? Are there some topics that reoccur, and how does the child's writing on these topics evolve over time? What does the child tend to do most often when he or she sits down to write? What patterns can one detect in how a child goes about starting a narrative? An entry that aims to become an essay? How does the child seem to keep him or herself going? What principles of elaboration are evident in the child's writing? How much of the child's writing seems to be done in school? At home? What sorts of topics or genre or conditions seem to generate energy for the child?

One of the most important things to look for is this: to what extent do we see evidence that instruction is effecting what the child does? Obviously, children sometimes will be influenced by instruction without necessarily using the instruction toward fruitful ends. But it is still very important simply to look for evidence that instruction is having an effect on children's writing.

If in all of this assessment we see that synapses are broken between teaching and learning, or we see that some children are not making palpable progress, then it is important to ask "why?" Similarly, when we see that our teaching is absolutely making a difference in some children's writing, and if we let children know this (and let them know that we know), their growth takes off and along the way and we stand a chance of hitching some wagons to those stars!

Goals and Rubrics

It is also important that teachers and children work toward clearly-specified goals within a unit of study and throughout the year. Of course, end-of-year standards need to inform the day-to-day decisions we make as we teach. To that end, we have specified clear goals for each unit of study, goals that help us assess each child and our own teaching

within each unit. You'll find a rubric in each *Unit of Study*, and all of them are on the accompanying CD-ROM.

The rubrics provided with the units are intended to serve two purposes. First, they name the intentions we have for writers in our classrooms as we move through the various units. Second, they encourage us to step back and see the commonalities across units—the "big ideas" in writing that are embodied in the series as a whole.

We strongly encourage you to make these documents your own. Working with colleagues, adapt them to the goals you have for the children in your care and use this format as an opportunity to talk and write about what matters to you as a learning community.

Writing Conferences

Although assessment weaves through every moment of our teaching, we especially assess during one-to-one writing conferences. For many years, teachers in our community carried clipboards with them and scrawled anecdotal notes about the child's topic, genre, and process decisions. Recently, however, we studied those anecdotal notes and found that sometimes the expectation that we must keep records during our conferences distracts us from feeling duty-bound to teach the child something during these interactions. We can find ourselves dutifully recording whatever the child says in a conference and then moving on, oblivious to our not having taught the child anything. In order to make it more likely that our conferences actually provide teaching opportunities, we have recently begun speculating in advance on the sorts of things we will watch for in order to see what children do. We watch with a record sheet in hand, and if children do something we regard as significant to the unit, we make note of it. If we teach the child a particular skill or strategy, then we record a *T* (for teaching) and hope that in the days ahead we'll observe (and record) the child doing this independently. In this way, our record sheet of the conferences we hold with individuals also records what individual writers are able to do.

Assessment is not an end in itself. Assessment must be purposeful to be either effective or useful. If our notes and files stay in the drawer or on the shelf gathering dust, they have been for naught. They need to be brought into the public eye from time to time to show what children can learn to do when given the chance. They are the evidence that allows us to teach in the ways we know are best for children. Static assessment files have their purpose in allowing us to be held accountable to others and ourselves for our teaching. But changing, growing assessment notes are most useful to our teaching and learning. When we take what we learn about our students and use that information to teach them more, teach them differently, place them in helpful learning contexts, and show them how their hard work has made a difference in their ability to make sense of and participate in the world, then our assessment has truly been worthy of us and worthy of our students.

APPENDIX

Frequently Asked Questions About This Series . . . And Some Answers

Has this curriculum been piloted?

The units of study described in the two series of books—*Units of Study for Primary Writing*, and *Units of Study for Teaching Writing, Grades 3–5*—grew from the Teachers College Reading and Writing Project's deep, intensive and long-lasting affiliation with thousands of schools across the nation and the world. For almost three decades, my colleagues and I at the Project have collaboratively developed ideas on the teaching of writing, and then helped teachers and school leaders bring those ideas to classrooms and schools where, in turn, we learn from the young writers who help us outgrow our best-draft ideas about the teaching of writing. This cycle of curriculum development, teaching, action-research, assessment, and curricular revision has meant that for almost thirty years, those of us who are affiliated with the remarkable community that coalesces around the Teachers College Reading and Writing Project have been able to stand on the shoulders of work that has gone before us.

When the leadership of New York City decided several years ago to bring the writing workshop to every classroom throughout the city, I knew that teachers would need extra curricular support. At the Teachers College Reading and Writing Project, we wrote incomplete, fast-draft versions of these units of study and distributed them in loose-leaf binders. I gave schools throughout New York City approximately 30,000 binders, each containing several hundred pages. These were trucked to the elementary and middle schools which ascribe to our Project's work. For three years now, we have watched those materials be translated into teaching and learning, and have continuously revised our thinking based on what we have learned. So yes, the series has been piloted.

Is there scientifically-based data vouching for the effectiveness of these curricular materials?

The only assessment measure that has been used for many years (thirty) and has been used across every state is the NAEP (National Assessment of Educational Progress). The NAEP has often been referred to as "the nation's report card," and it has been used to compare and contrast different state exams. Several years ago the NAEP assessment found that New York City's children write as well or better than children in every other major city except Charlotte (New Yorkers jokingly question whether Charlotte qualifies as a *major* city!).

Across the nation, NAEP scores have been basically unchanging for thirty years. The current administration declared a triumph when this year's national average rose 1%. Meanwhile, scores in New York City rose a dramatic 7%, since the city's leadership brought balanced literacy and assessment-based reading interventions to scale. New York City's African-American students and English Language Learners improved in even more dramatic ways. According to the NAEP, New York City's lower income African-American and Latino children far outperformed similar studies in large cities in the nation as a whole.

From 2005 until now, NAEP has disaggregated data to show progress in ten large urban cities. From the first data point in 2002 until the most recent data in 2005, New York City has made a 10% gain. Sheila Ford, who announced the NAEP scores in a press conference in Boston, said, "This is a very significant gain." It is particularly important to bear in mind that meanwhile, New York City has 1.1 million children with 85% of them eligible for free and reduced lunch.

There is a great deal of data suggesting that improvements in writing will have a payoff across the curriculum.

If a school or district adopts the two series—*Units of Study for Primary Writing* and *Units of Study for Teaching Writing, Grades 3-5*—will the books within these series be enough to sustain children's growth and teachers' instruction across all the grades?

The answer to this is no. These series of books were never intended to replace all the professional reading and study that teachers have been doing for all these years! You and your colleagues will absolutely need to continue to read other professional books, and you will need to continue to author your own ideas as well.

But yes, the two series of books can provide the *backbone* to a K–5 approach to the teaching of writing, bringing coherence to your school-wide or district-wide writing curriculum.

These books absolutely support a spiral curriculum. For example, the books can help teachers of kindergartners to support children as they begin drawing, labeling, telling and writing simple Small Moment stories—and then over the years, the books will help teachers equip children to use more and more complex concepts, tools and strategies so that by fifth grade, children are not only writing sophisticated stories, they are also embedding those stories in memoir and personal essays, and using techniques developed in personal narrative to write short fiction. In a similar fashion, this spiraling curriculum supports teachers in scaffolding children's writing of expository and informational texts.

The truth is that at no point will the books suffice as a script for your teaching. They are a very detailed model. They convey the story of what I (and in some instances, what colleagues of mine) did in order to teach a unit of study to a particular group of children. The books are filled with examples of my writing, with anecdotes about my dog and my family, and they are filled also with examples that come from particular children. Teachers at every grade level in a school will need to revise these lessons so they reflect you and your particular children, and so they are tailored to what your children can almost do. This means that when third-grade teachers, fourth-grade teachers, then fifth-grade teachers all rely on the books, you will at every point need to bring yourself and your kids to this model.

But if you ask whether, in general, it is appropriate for third graders to proceed through these units and then for fourth graders to revisit these units, and for fifth graders to have yet another go at them, the answer is usually yes. It is like learning to play tennis. You work on serving the ball when you are starting to learn, and again when you have been playing tennis for a year, and you still continue to work on serving the ball when you are a member of a varsity tennis team. In a similar manner, those of us who write continue to work at the same challenges, year after year. I find that the lessons I teach to third graders are very much the same lessons, tweaked a bit, that I teach to graduate students, and then when I get a bit of time, alone at my desk, these are the lessons I teach myself.

If I teach children who have not grown up within a writing workshop, can I follow these units of study? Or do they require a foundation that I will need to provide children?

If your children did not participate in a writing workshop before this year, you will certainly want to start with *Launching the Writing Workshop* and proceed (for the most part) in sequence. The truth is that you will want to do this even if your children did have the benefits of a writing workshop throughout their primary grades! So the answer to your concerns is this: Don't worry. Carry on! These units were designed, knowing that this would be the case for many teachers and children.

How much time should I devote to a single unit of study? If my children do not write particularly well, or if I am new to the teaching of writing, should I extend the time frame?

These units are designed to support a month-long unit of study. If you or your children are new to writing workshop, then you should expect to progress more quickly, not more slowly, through a unit of study. That is, when your children are skilled and experienced writers, they'll be able to spend more time revising and improving their draft, but if they are less experienced (or if you are), they'll probably stay closer to the pathway I've laid out.

Which books and other materials do I need to purchase to support these units of study?

There is a chapter in this book which describes the pens, folders, paper and notebooks that your children will need. On the CD-ROM included with the series, you will find resources you'll use and suggestions for texts or additional materials organized on a session-by-session (day-by-day) basis. Of course, you'll want to be sure to have some children's literature. The texts that are referred to the most in this series include Sandra Cisneros' and *House on Mango Street*, Cynthia Rylant's *Every Living Thing*, an anthology of short stories, the picture books *Fireflies!* by Julie Brinkloe and *Peter's Chair* by Ezra Jack Keats.